# Tana Ramsay's
## real
## family food

For Gordon. Thank you for being you.

■ HarperCollins*Publishers*

HarperCollins*Publishers*
77–85 Fulham Palace Road
Hammersmith, London W6 8JB

www.harpercollins.co.uk

First published by HarperCollins 2007

10 9 8 7 6 5 4 3 2

© Tana Ramsay 2007

Tana Ramsay asserts the moral right to
be identified as the author of this work

Photographs © Deirdre Rooney

Styling: Wei Tang
Food styling: Jenny White
Home economist: Alexandra Howard

A catalogue record of this book is
available from the British Library

ISBN-13   978-0-00-725933-5
ISBN-10   0-00-725933-6

Printed and bound in Great Britain by
Butler and Tanner, Somerset

This book includes reference to nuts and recipes including nuts,
nut derivatives and nut oils. Avoid if you have a known allergic reaction.
Pregnant and nursing mothers, invalids, the elderly, children and babies
may be potentially vulnerable to nut allergies and should therefore avoid
nuts, nut derivatives and nut oils.

# contents

# introduction

This year we celebrated Megan's ninth birthday and, like many parents, Gordon and I couldn't help wondering how so much time could feel like so little. Even our youngest, Tilly, is five now and she's meant to be the baby of the family!

With the children getting older, I've noticed that what I cook for them has become more grown up too. Although I still add very little salt to my cooking and hold back on hot spices, what I cook the children for tea will nearly always work later as dinner for Gordon and me. This is why I've tried to make the recipes in *Real Family Food* as tempting for adults as they are for children. It also has the added bonus of only having to think about one dinner in the evenings, not two (I call it convenience, not laziness!).

When you think about it, ultimately we only need to eat to refuel and keep ourselves going throughout the day. Even so, I believe that food can play another, almost more important, part in our lives. It can bring us together, slow us down and let us catch up with each other as we rush through the week. Some of the happiest moments of my life have been around the table sharing good food, and the times I treasure most with my family are when we are all together doing just that. This must be why I associate certain foods and dishes with different people and places. For example, blueberry muffins always make me think of my sister as she's so addicted to them, calamari bring back memories of baking hot holidays in the south of France, and the smell of Moroccan lamb cooking takes me right back to Sunday mornings in the kitchen with my mum. It's memories like these that make me smile. It's a bit like a song making you think of someone. I'm willing to bet that different foods conjure up different memories for you too.

Food brings people together, especially families. The more we can get together around the table and share each other's company, the closer and more strongly knit we can become – even on the days when nobody can agree on anything!

With this in mind, I've tried to organize the recipes in this book around everyday social occasions – from hurried weekday breakfasts and leisurely family get-togethers to picnics in parks and casual lunches with friends.

For example, 'Breakfasts and Brunches' has some very quick and easy ideas to put together during the week, as well as other more leisurely brunch options for lazy Saturday or Sunday mornings when you can't be bothered to get out of your pyjamas. Similarly, 'Food in a Flash' is designed for frantic evenings when everybody is piling through the door and clamouring for dinner, your attention and general sanity. By contrast, 'Laid-back Suppers' is for those evenings when you have a little more time on your hands. Most of these take slightly more time to prepare, but once they're in the oven you can usually leave them to take care of themselves.

Probably my favourite section is 'Picnics and Treats'. My kids like nothing more than eating outside, and I'm pretty sure that some of their best food memories must be tied up in outdoor parties with family and friends.

Vegetables are arguably not an event in themselves, but I know that sometimes they can feel like one! Children have a tendency to dig in their heels over allowing one or two peas to fall on their plates, let alone finishing them up. My lot still need encouragement when it comes to eating their greens, but I've always tried to see it as a positive challenge and, with a bit of trial and error, I've found ways to make them think that vegetables are okay after all. Hopefully, they'll go down well with your family too.

Whilst we're on the subject of experimentation, the section of recipes called 'Try Something Different' is designed to let you and your family do just that. Again, it's not, strictly speaking, organized around an occasion, but it's designed to encourage your children to enjoy different food flavours so that if you go out for dinner, either to different styles of restaurant or abroad on holiday, they're not fazed by what arrives on their plates.

For the days when you've got the in-laws descending on you in droves, the recipes in 'Big Family Lunches' should be able to help you stay calm amidst the general chaos. Most of these can be prepared in advance and then left in the oven or pot to cook, so you should end up having plenty of time to get ready yourself. Serve these with one or two of the vegetable side dishes in 'Vegetable Temptations' and follow up with one of the 'Devilish Desserts' and you can't fail to impress!

Finally, you may notice that I've tended not to recommend what you should eat with what, for example which side dishes should be eaten with which main courses, or which desserts works best with which lunches (unless I have a real favourite). I've done this deliberately as I believe you should be able to eat anything you like in whatever combination you like. I think we've become too worried about doing everything right and getting everything officially perfect. Life's too short! We need to relax and trust our instincts more. I think this is how we can learn the most about food and cooking, and it's certainly how I learnt. Besides, if I worried the whole time about being perfect, then Gordon would never get fed at all!

So trust yourself, relax and enjoy bringing your family together again and again with simple, satisfying food. In years to come they'll have all sorts of amazing memories tied up with the food you cooked and the times you shared together.

# Breakfasts and Brunches

Weekdays always go past in a blur. If I'm not rushing out the door to get the kids to school on time, I'm trying to figure out where I'm meant to be next. By the time it gets to the weekend, there is nothing I like more than a long lazy morning.

The children have finally got the hang of lie-ins, so when we eventually get downstairs (still in our pyjamas of course) we're all ready for a hearty breakfast. These are the mornings I treasure the most with my family.

Yoghurt and berry crunch

Porridge with almond roasted peaches

Oat and blueberry muffins

Pecan and bran banana muffins

Bacon and egg muffins

Grilled mackerel on toast

Avocado, bacon and roasted tomato sandwich

Cinnamon eggy bread soldiers with yoghurt, raisins and honey

Salmon and dill frittata

Smoked haddock pots

Croque Madame

Smoked salmon, cream cheese and scrambled egg bagels

Homemade bagels

# yoghurt and berry crunch

*I make these in little glass tumblers from Ikea as they tend to bounce when dropped and are fabulously childproof!*

370g/13oz frozen berries
1 tbsp brown sugar
10 digestive biscuits
370g/13oz Greek yoghurt

1  Place the berries in a small saucepan with the sugar and cook over a low heat until they become a soft, pulpy mess. Remove from the heat and allow to cool.

2  Crush the digestive biscuits with the back of a spoon.

3  Place a 1cm/½ inch layer of crushed digestives into the bottom of each glass. Spoon 1cm/½ inch of the Greek yoghurt on top, followed by 1cm/½ inch of the fruit. Repeat this so you have 6 layers in total (2 of each). Serve immediately or refrigerate for later.

**Makes:** 4 × 100ml/4fl oz tumblers
**Prep time:** 15 minutes
**Cooking time:** 10–15 minutes

TIP

■  To save time, cook the berries the day before you need them.

# porridge with almond-roasted peaches

*This is really easy to make before school while the children are getting dressed.*
*Perfect for a winter morning pick-me-up.*

25g/1oz butter
4 peaches, halved, stones removed
25g/1oz soft brown sugar
75g/3oz flaked almonds
100g/4oz porridge oats
600ml/1 pint whole milk
300ml/11fl oz water

1  Preheat the oven to 180°C/350°F/GM4.

2  Generously butter a small ovenproof dish and arrange the peaches in it, cut side uppermost.
   It should be quite a snug fit, with the peaches bumping up against each other. Place in
   the oven and set the timer for 7 minutes.

3  Mix together the soft brown sugar and flaked almonds and put to one side.

4  Put the oats, milk and water into a medium-sized saucepan and bring to the boil, stirring
   all the time. Turn down the heat and simmer for about 7 minutes until the porridge is
   thick and creamy.

5  When the oven timer beeps, sprinkle the peaches with the almonds and sugar and return
   to the oven for a further 10 minutes.

6  Divide the porridge between 4 bowls and arrange 2 peach halves on top of each. Spoon
   over the syrupy almonds and serve immediately.

**Serves:** 4 children
**Prep time:** 20 minutes, depending on ripeness of peaches
**Cooking time:** 17 minutes

TIPS

■ Nectarines and apricots work well too.

■ You can soak the oats overnight in milk or fruit juice to save time in the morning.

# oat and blueberry muffins

Blueberry muffins have always been a favourite treat for breakfast in my house, and my sister is seriously addicted to them, as are her two children. I usually have to bulk-bake when I make these...

340g/12oz self-raising flour
150g/5oz light brown sugar
25g/1oz porridge oats (plus 15g/½oz extra for sprinkling)
180ml/6½fl oz buttermilk
125ml/4½fl oz vegetable oil
150g/5oz fresh blueberries (frozen and defrosted is fine
    if you can't find fresh berries)
1 egg, beaten

1 Preheat the oven to 180°C/350°F/GM4.

2 Place 12 paper cases into a muffin tin.

3 Sieve the flour into a large mixing bowl, add the sugar and oats and mix thoroughly. Add the buttermilk, egg and vegetable oil, mix through then stir in the blueberries, taking care not to crush them.

4 Spoon the mixture into the muffin cases, dividing it equally between them. Sprinkle the extra oats on top and place in the oven for 15–20 minutes until golden and firm to the touch.

5 Remove from the oven and transfer to a wire cooling rack.

**Makes:** 12 muffins
**Prep time:** 15 minutes
**Cooking time:** 15–20 minutes

TIP

■ You could replace the blueberries with raspberries if you prefer.

# pecan and bran banana muffins

These substantial muffins are a superb grab-and-go breakfast. They are also a delicious addition to any lunchbox and a great energy booster for children before after-school activities. They'll keep well for up to two days.

100g/4oz butter, softened
100g/4oz soft light brown sugar
3 nice and ripe bananas, mashed
60ml/2fl oz milk
1 tsp vanilla extract
2 eggs, beaten

300g/10½oz plain flour
100g/4oz bran flakes
1 tsp baking powder
¼ tsp salt
1 tsp baking soda
200g/7oz finely chopped pecans

1 Preheat the oven to 190°C/375°F/GM5.

2 Mix together the butter and sugar until light and fluffy. Add the mashed bananas, milk, vanilla and eggs and stir together well. Stir in the remaining ingredients, mixing all through.

3 Spoon the mixture into 12 paper muffin cases, dividing it equally between them.

4 Place in a muffin tin and bake for 25–30 minutes. Remove and place on a cooling rack.

**Makes:** 12 muffins
**Prep time:** 15 minutes
**Cooking time:** 25–30 minutes

# bacon and egg muffins

*These breakfast muffins are a meal in themselves. Filling but extremely moreish!*

340g/12oz self-raising flour
100g/4oz butter, chopped
2 tsp mustard powder
pinch of Maldon sea salt
1 small onion, very finely chopped

1 egg, lightly beaten
250ml/9fl oz milk
10 rashers unsmoked streaky bacon
10 quail eggs
10 × 1cm/½ inch cubes of butter

1  Preheat the oven to 180°C/350°F/GM4.

2  Sieve the flour and rub together with the chopped butter, leaving the mixture a little rough. Stir in the mustard powder, salt, chopped onion, beaten egg and milk and mix thoroughly.

3  Grill the bacon and cut into small pieces (approximately 1cm/½ inch). Combine with the muffin mixture.

4  Divide the mixture equally between 10 paper muffin cases.

5  Make a deep well in the centre of the muffin mixture within each paper case and crack in one of the quail eggs. Then pull the muffin mixture so that it almost covers the egg and place a butter cube on top to stop the egg going hard. Repeat with the other muffins and eggs.

6  Bake in a muffin tin for 15–20 minutes, checking regularly.

7  When golden, remove the muffins immediately and transfer to a wire cooling rack.

**Makes:** 10 muffins
**Prep time:** 15 minutes
**Cooking time:** 15–20 minutes

# grilled mackerel on toast

High in protein, vitamins and omega-3 fats, mackerel is a real superfood. A bonus is that it is both cheap and delicious, and children really seem to enjoy the smoky taste of the fish. This recipe is quick and easy to prepare, making it an ideal alternative to toast and honey on a school morning!

2 smoked mackerel fillets, weighing
   approximately 250g/9oz, skinned
4 pieces good quality wholemeal bread
1 tbsp crème fraîche
2 tsp horseradish sauce
25g/1oz chives, finely chopped
pepper

1 Put the mackerel fillets on a baking sheet and place under a hot grill.

2 Meanwhile, toast the bread and mix together the crème fraîche, horseradish and chopped chives, seasoning well with pepper.

3 After about 5 minutes the mackerel will be bubbling and beginning to colour. Remove from the grill and roughly flake.

4 Cut each piece of toast into 4 triangles. Top each triangle with smoked mackerel and a dollop of the crème fraîche mixture and serve immediately.

**Serves:** 4 children
**Prep time:** 10 minutes
**Cooking time:** 5 minutes

# avocado, bacon and roasted tomato sandwich

*This is definitely one of my favourite brunch options – particularly for the lunchtime end of brunch.*

1 large plum tomato, sliced
½ tsp dried oregano
pinch of Maldon sea salt
freshly ground black pepper
3 rashers of bacon (I like maple best, but any
    good quality unsmoked bacon will do)
2 thick slices of wholemeal bread
scraping of butter for each slice
½ avocado, nice and ripe, thinly sliced lengthways

1  Preheat the oven to 190°C/375°F/GM5.

2  Lightly grease an oven tray. Place the tomato slices on the tray, sprinkling over the dried oregano, salt and a twist of black pepper. Place in the oven for approximately 20 minutes, turning once.

3  While the tomatoes are in the oven, grill the bacon until slightly crisp so it contrasts nicely with the soft avocado and tomato.

4  Lightly toast the bread and spread with the butter. Lay on the slices of avocado followed by the bacon and topped by the tomatoes. Place the other piece of toast on top, slice and serve.

5  Delicious with mayonnaise added but healthier without.

**Serves:** 1
**Prep time:** 15 minutes
**Cooking time:** 20 minutes

# cinnamon eggy bread soldiers with yoghurt, raisins and honey

*This makes a fabulous, very quick start to a busy school day. Naughty but nice!*

3 eggs
100ml/4fl oz double cream
100ml/4fl oz milk
½ tsp ground cinnamon
4 pieces thick-sliced white bread
275g/10oz butter for frying
300ml/11fl oz Greek yoghurt
300g/10½oz raisins
4 tbsp runny honey

1 Whisk together the eggs, cream, milk and cinnamon.

2 Dip each piece of bread in the mixture and stack on a plate.

3 Heat half the butter in a large frying pan (preferably non-stick). When the butter is very hot, add 2 of the bread pieces and fry for 2–3 minutes on each side until golden brown.

4 Put on a plate and keep warm while you melt the rest of the butter and begin the process again.

5 Cut each piece of bread into 5 soldiers and serve beside a dollop of Greek yoghurt sprinkled with raisins.

6 Drizzle honey over everything and serve immediately.

**Serves:** 4 children
**Prep time:** 5 minutes
**Cooking time:** 10–15 minutes

TIPS

■ This is better made with slightly stale bread, which means it's a great way of using up an old loaf.

■ My frying pan isn't large enough to do four slices of bread at once so I make it in two batches, but because it cooks so quickly, nobody seems to notice.

# salmon and dill frittata

This is an ideal weekend brunch if you've got some friends coming round.
I like it best served with some green salad and thick wedges of fresh wholemeal
bread. You could also try making this in the morning for a lunchtime picnic –
it tastes wonderful at room temperature and makes a great alternative to
soggy sandwiches!

500g/18oz salmon fillet, skinned
1 bay leaf
6 peppercorns
1 medium onion, finely chopped
1 potato (approximately 275g/10oz), diced
3 tsp olive oil for frying
6 eggs
250ml/9fl oz double cream
25g/1oz bunch dill, stalks removed and
   finely chopped
salt and pepper

1 Preheat the grill to hot (approximately 240°C/475°F).

2 Place the salmon in a medium saucepan with the bay leaf and peppercorns. Cover with water and bring to the boil. Put on the lid and leave to simmer for 10 minutes. Turn off the heat. Using a slotted spoon, remove the salmon, flake into a bowl and allow to cool.

3 In a 25cm/10 inch circular cast-iron dish or non-stick frying pan, sweat the onion and potato in the olive oil by covering with a large plate or tin foil and cooking on a low heat. After 25 minutes the onion should be translucent and the potato just cooked.

4 While the potatoes are cooking, whisk together the eggs, cream and dill. Lightly season – this does tend to need a little salt.

5 When the potato and onion are ready, add the flaked salmon and pour the cream mixture over them. Turn up the heat a little and cook gently for 10 minutes or until the egg has started to set.

6 At this point, if you are using a frying pan, make sure the handle is well covered with tin foil so that it won't melt under the grill.

7 Remove the frittata from the hob and place under the grill for 2–3 minutes until golden. The top of the frittata should be about 10cm/4 inches from the grill element – any closer and it will burn.

8 Remove from the heat and allow to stand for at least 10 minutes before cutting into slices and serving.

**Serves:** 4
**Prep time:** 20 minutes
**Cooking time:** 40 minutes
**Standing time:** 10 minutes

**TIP**

- If you're not a fan of dill you could substitute with a small bunch of finely chopped chives or parsley.

- Adding red peppers or peas to the frittata not only adds a splash of colour but is also a sneaky way of adding a few extra vegetables!

# smoked haddock pots

*These are incredibly easy and make a really delicious brunch when served with fresh wholemeal bread or crushed new potatoes.*

250g/9oz spinach
250ml/9fl oz double cream
100ml/4fl oz milk
1 tbsp wholegrain mustard
600g/21oz smoked haddock fillet, skinned
pepper
25g/1oz parsley, roughly chopped
1 lemon, quartered
wholemeal bread to serve

1 Preheat the oven to 180°C/350°F/GM4.

2 Wash the spinach thoroughly. Shake the water off and place in a large saucepan over a medium heat. Put the lid on the saucepan and cook until the spinach wilts. Drain in a colander and allow to cool.

3 Mix together the cream, milk and grain mustard and put to one side.

4 When the spinach is cool enough to handle, squeeze out as much water as possible using the back of a large metal spoon. Roughly chop the spinach and divide between the four 250ml/9fl oz ramekins.

5 Now divide the uncooked haddock between the ramekins, feeling for as many bones as possible and tweezering them out, and pour the cream mixture over the top. Season with pepper but not salt as the haddock will be salty enough already.

6 Bake for 20–25 minutes until the cream is really bubbling.

7 Remove from the oven and sprinkle with parsley. Squeeze the lemon over the top and serve immediately with wholemeal bread.

**Serves:** 4
**Prep time:** 20 minutes
**Cooking time:** 20–25 minutes

# croque madame

*This is a perfect Saturday morning breakfast for all the family and an excellent alternative to traditional bacon and eggs. It's also really easy to make.*

8 slices good quality thick-sliced white bread
200g/7oz Gruyère cheese, finely grated
12 slices smoked ham
50g/2oz butter, very soft
3 tbsp olive oil
3 tbsp sunflower oil
4 eggs

1 Preheat the grill to high (240ºC/475ºF).

2 Place 4 slices of bread on a baking tray and sprinkle with half the grated Gruyère.

3 Arrange 3 slices of ham on top then sprinkle over the remaining cheese. Cover with another slice of bread and push down firmly. Butter the top of each sandwich very thinly and put to one side for a moment while you prepare the eggs.

4 Heat the oils in a frying pan until very hot. Carefully crack the eggs into the oil and turn the heat down a little.

5 As soon as the eggs are in the pan, put the sandwiches under the grill. I always set the oven timer for 1 minute as it is easy to forget about them while you are concentrating on the eggs.

6 After 1–2 minutes the sandwiches will be a beautiful golden colour. Carefully flip them over, butter the other side and return them under the grill. Again, set the oven timer for a minute.

7 Returning to the eggs: carefully tip the frying pan to one side and, using a metal tablespoon, ladle the hot oil over the egg yolks. This will ensure that the eggs are runny in the centre but cooked on the top.

8 After 1–2 minutes the sandwiches will be golden on the other side. Remove from the grill and serve immediately with a fried egg on top of each.

**Serves:** 4
**Prep time:** 15 minutes
**Cooking time:** 10 minutes

# smoked salmon, cream cheese and scrambled egg bagels

Everyone has their own way of making scrambled eggs. Mine isn't perfect but it certainly goes down well in my house. If you're feeling virtuous and have lots of time on your hands you can also make your own bagels (see page 24).

4 bagels (bought or homemade)
soft cheese (I use Philadelphia),
    to spread
4 slices good smoked salmon
1 lemon, cut into wedges
black pepper

FOR THE SCRAMBLED EGGS
6 eggs
good pinch of Maldon sea salt
good grinding of black pepper
60ml/2fl oz milk (and a splash of cream
    for indulgence...)
knob of butter

1 Slice the bagels and put them in the toaster, ready to toast.

2 Crack all the eggs into a large mixing bowl, add the salt and pepper and the milk, and whisk together thoroughly.

3 In a large non-stick saucepan, melt the butter over a moderate heat. Add the egg mixture and stir continuously, stirring in any bits that catch on the side or at the bottom of the pan.

4 Pop the bagels down in the toaster to toast lightly. Remove and set aside.

5 Meanwhile, keep stirring the eggs for approximately 10 minutes until the mixture forms lumps and becomes scrambled. Remove from the heat slightly before it is ready and allow to stand for a minute or two. This stops it from overcooking which can happen very suddenly – you don't want dry scrambled eggs!

6 Spread each bagel half with soft cheese – be generous!

7 On 4 of the bagel halves place a slice of smoked salmon, squeeze over some lemon juice then top with scrambled egg and another good grinding of black pepper. Sandwich together with the other bagel halves and serve immediately.

**Serves:** 4
**Prep time:** 10 minutes
**Cooking time:** 10 minutes

# homemade bagels

*I nearly always buy fresh bagels as it involves far less effort, but if you're an early riser and fancy an adventure in the kitchen you can of course make your own. I've done it a few times – it's fun but time-consuming.*

3 tbsp dry yeast
2 tbsp caster sugar
125ml/4½fl oz warm water
   (plus 1 tsp to add later)
250ml/9fl oz warm milk
450g/1lb plain flour, sieved

3 tsp salt
1 egg yolk
1 tbsp poppy seeds or sesame seeds
   (whichever you prefer)
2 tsp Maldon sea salt

1 Put the yeast, 1 tbsp of the caster sugar, the water and milk into a large mixing bowl and whisk together until all the yeast is dissolved. Cover and leave in a warm place for 10–15 minutes until it is beginning to bubble.

2 Add the flour, salt and the remaining 1 tbsp of caster sugar (with the dough hook if using a mixer) and mix to a firm dough. This shouldn't be too sticky – adjust by adding a little extra flour if needed.

3 Turn the dough out onto a floured surface and knead for 5–10 minutes until it is really smooth and elastic.

4 Place the dough into a large bowl, cover with a damp tea towel and stand in a warm place for approximately 1 hour until it has doubled in size. Be careful not to leave it for too long or it will form a hard crust on the top which stops it rising properly.

5 Flour the work surface and turn out your dough. Knead it a little more then divide into 10 equal balls.

6 Using your finger, make a hole in the middle of each ball and massage into a bagel shape. The hole in the centre should be approximately 2½cm/1 inch in diameter and there should be equal thickness in the edges all around. Resist perfection at this point or you'll go mad!

7   Place your 10 bagels onto a greased baking sheet, cover with a damp tea towel and leave in a warm place for 20 minutes to give them a chance to rise again.

8   Preheat the oven to 190°C/375°F/GM5.

9   Bring to the boil a large pan of water, lower the bagels in batches into the water and blanch for 1 minute. Remove and place back onto the lightly greased baking sheet.

10  Brush over the tops of the bagels with the egg yolk and sprinkle over your chosen seeds.

11  Bake for 20 minutes until golden then cool on a wire rack.

**Makes:** 10 bagels
**Prep time:** 2 hours, including rising time
**Cooking time:** 5–10 minutes to blanch the bagels
and 20 minutes to bake

TIP

■   It's easiest to make the dough in a food mixer with a whisk attachment, followed by a dough hook. By hand is also fine, just slightly harder work!

# Light Lunches

No matter how much you vary the fillings, sandwiches can get really monotonous! I'm often trying to come up with different ideas for lunch that won't take too long to prepare. These are all ideas I've fallen back on in the past. Many of them will work in lunchboxes and can be made the evening before (for more lunchbox ideas, see Picnics and Treats). They are also ideal for informal lunches with friends when you'd rather be catching up on all the gossip than spending hours in the kitchen.

Hearty winter soup

Chilled cucumber and mint gazpacho

Chicken skewers with sweet and sour sauce

Red onion tarte tatin

Ham and cheese roll-ups

Salmon fishcakes

Lamb samosas

Mackerel salad with beetroot and horseradish dressing

Warm potato, chorizo and parsley salad

# hearty winter soup

What could be more essential than a flask of hot soup when standing on a football sideline on a Saturday afternoon in the freezing cold? The chilli flakes give added heat which I swear can bring back the feeling in your toes. Quinoa (pronounced 'keen-wah') is rapidly becoming known as a superfood because it's a complete protein containing all eight amino acids. It's increasingly available in supermarkets and can be used as a substitute for rice.

3 tbsp olive oil
1 red onion, finely diced
1 garlic clove, crushed
1 fennel bulb, finely chopped
2 sticks celery, finely chopped
1 courgette, finely diced
2 carrots, finely diced
50g/2oz quinoa
1 × 400g/14oz tin chopped tomatoes

800ml/28fl oz water
1 quality chicken stock cube
¼ tsp chilli flakes
1 × 400g/14oz tin mixed beans
large bunch flat-leaf parsley, finely
    chopped
1 lemon, juiced
salt and pepper
grated Parmesan (optional)

1  Heat the olive oil in a large saucepan. Fry the onion until it starts to soften. Add the garlic and other chopped vegetables and fry for a further 5 minutes or so.

2  Add the quinoa followed by the tinned tomatoes, water and stock cube.

3  Add the chilli flakes and stir well.

4  Simmer for 15 minutes with the lid on before adding the beans. Simmer for a further 10 minutes.

5  Add the parsley and lemon juice. Season well with salt and pepper.

6  Drink from a flask or in warm bowls sprinkled with grated Parmesan.

**Makes:** a large flask
**Prep time:** 20 minutes
**Cooking time:** 40 minutes

# chilled cucumber and mint gazpacho

*A light and refreshing summer option – serve in mugs for children. Mine particularly like adding extra mint leaves of their own.*

4 large cucumbers
100ml/4fl oz olive oil
5 ice cubes
5–6 sprigs of fresh mint
1 small garlic clove, finely sliced
salt and pepper, to taste
dash of full-cream milk
2 tsp horseradish

1 Peel and remove the seeds of 3 of the cucumbers, leaving 1 with seeds and the skin on for good colour. Roughly chop them and place in a large bowl with the olive oil, ice cubes, mint, garlic and salt and pepper.

2 Cover the top of the bowl with cling film and leave to marinate in the fridge for at least 4 hours.

3 Place all ingredients from the bowl into a blender and add the milk and horseradish. Blend until completely smooth and check the seasoning, adding as necessary.

4 Keep chilled until just before serving.

**Makes:** 3 large or 6 small portions
**Prep time:** ½ hour
**Marinating time:** 4 hours

TIP

- For an extra treat, fry a little pancetta until crunchy, then sprinkle on top.

# chicken skewers with sweet and sour sauce

These taste just as good cold as they do hot so they make a great addition to a packed lunch.

2 skinless chicken breasts

FOR THE MARINADE
3 limes, juiced
2 tbsp soy sauce
1 tbsp sesame oil
1 tbsp runny honey

FOR THE SWEET AND SOUR SAUCE
150ml/5fl oz water
2 tbsp sugar
3 tbsp Chinese rice vinegar
3 tbsp tomato ketchup
1 tsp salt
2 tsp cornflour mixed with 2 tsp water

1  Preheat the oven to 180°C/350°F/GM4.

2  Soak 8 wooden skewers in water.

3  Mix together all the marinade ingredients in a medium bowl and put to one side.

4  Put the chicken breasts between two pieces of clingfilm and bash with a rolling pin until they have doubled in size.

5  Cut the chicken into strips about 1cm/½ inch wide and put them into the marinade.

6  Cover the chicken with clingfilm and leave overnight in the fridge (or for about 2 hours at room temperature).

7  Meanwhile, make the sweet and sour sauce by putting all the ingredients, except the cornflour mixture, into a saucepan and bringing to the boil. Stir in the cornflour mixture and simmer for a couple of minutes. Allow to cool.

8  When you are ready to cook the chicken, carefully weave the strips of chicken onto the skewers and place on a baking rack.

9  Cook for 15 minutes, turning the skewers over once during this time.

**Makes:** 8 kebabs
**Prep time:** 30 minutes (plus 2 hours to marinate at room temperature)
**Cooking time:** 15 minutes

# red onion tarte tatin

50g/2oz butter
1 tbsp caster sugar
500g/18oz red onions, peeled and halved
1 tbsp balsamic vinegar
150g/5oz fresh, soft goats' cheese
2 tbsp chopped thyme
375g/13oz pack puff pastry

1 Generously grease a 25cm/10 inch tarte tatin tin or circular enamel dish with the butter. Sprinkle evenly with caster sugar. Tightly arrange the halved onions in the dish, cut side downwards.

2 Place on the hob over a low heat until the butter has melted. Increase the heat slightly and continue cooking for about 30 minutes or until the onions and butter are golden brown.

3 Pour over the balsamic vinegar and remove from the heat.

4 Preheat the oven to 180°C/350°F/GM4.

5 Allow the onions to cool a little before placing spoonfuls of the soft goats' cheese between them.

6 Sprinkle with half the chopped thyme.

7 Roll out the pastry and cut a circle about 4cm/1½ inches larger in diameter than the dish.

8 Lay the pastry on top of the onions and carefully tuck the edge down the sides of the dish.

9 Place in the preheated oven and cook for 40 minutes until the pastry is golden.

10 Remove from the oven and carefully turn out onto a serving dish.

11 Serve immediately sprinkled with the remaining thyme.

Serves: 6
Prep time: 20 minutes
Cooking time: 1 hour 10 minutes

# ham and cheese roll-ups

When the children are at home for lunch I sometimes like to do something different, and this is a great way of serving a simple hot lunch. The fillings can be as simple or as complicated as you like. I usually serve the roll-ups with a simple potato salad – boil some new potatoes, halve them and mix with chopped spring onions and mayonnaise.

400g/14oz puff pastry
50g/2oz mature cheese, grated
4 slices honey roast ham, cut into strips
6 cherry tomatoes, sliced

1  Preheat the oven to 190ºC/375ºF/GM5.

2  Roll out the pastry into a rectangle approximately ½ cm/¼ inch thick. Sprinkle over the grated cheese, covering the whole area. Layer over the strips of ham and sliced tomatoes.

3  Roll the pastry rectangle from the long edge into a sausage shape.

4  Bake for 15–20 minutes, until nicely golden.

5  Slice into 5cm/2 inch pieces. Be careful to allow to cool a little before eating as the cheese becomes very hot!

Serves: 4
Prep time: 15 minutes
Cooking time: 15–20 minutes

TIP

■ My favourite alternative fillings are tuna, mayonnaise and sweetcorn or cream cheese, ham and chives.

# salmon fishcakes

These delicious fishcakes taste great cold and can be made from store cupboard ingredients, so there's no excuse for not packing something more interesting than a cheese sandwich in a lunchbox! When I make this recipe, I always freeze half the mixture before shaping the rest into cakes. It's also a great way to use up leftover mashed potato.

2 anchovy fillets, finely chopped
450g/1lb tinned salmon
25g/1oz parsley, chopped
400g/14oz mashed potato
2 tbsp mayonnaise
1 egg, beaten
4 tbsp white breadcrumbs
25g/1oz butter for frying
2 tbsp sunflower oil

1 Finely chop the anchovy fillets before combining with the tinned salmon, parsley, mashed potato and mayonnaise. Try not to break the salmon up too much – I always think a chunky texture tastes better.

2 Pour in the egg and gently mix through.

3 Divide the mixture in 2 and put 1 half into a freezer bag to freeze for future use.

4 Shape into either 12 large balls or 24 small ones (smaller ones are ideal for lunchboxes).

5 Roll the balls in the breadcrumbs and squash flat.

6 Melt the butter and oil in a frying pan over a medium heat. When you think it's hot enough, throw a couple of breadcrumbs into the pan – if they immediately sizzle and colour, carefully place the fishcakes in the hot fat. Fry carefully for about 8 minutes, turning regularly to make sure both sides are cooked evenly and are nicely golden without being burnt.

**Makes:** 12 large or 24 small fishcakes
**Prep time:** 20 minutes
**Cooking time:** 8 minutes

# lamb samosas

*These samosas are brilliant in a lunchbox or as an after-school snack.*

2 tbsp olive oil
1 medium onion, finely chopped
1 tsp cumin seeds
500g/18oz minced lamb
2 tsp dried oregano
75g/3oz feta cheese, cut into 1cm/½ inch cubes
200g/7oz pack filo pastry

1 Preheat the oven to 180°C/350°F/GM4.

2 Heat 1 tbsp of olive oil in a frying pan and gently cook the onion until soft. Add the cumin seeds and fry for a further minute.

3 Increase the heat and add the lamb. As it begins to brown, break it up with a wooden spoon and fry until the juices have evaporated or you will have horrible, soggy samosas!

4 When the meat and onions are dry, cook for a few more minutes to allow the meat to brown slightly but watch carefully to make sure it doesn't burn. Tip it into a large mixing bowl and allow to cool slightly. Stir in the dried oregano and feta cheese, allowing the cheese to break down a bit while you mix.

5 Each sheet of filo pastry makes 1 samosa. Carefully brush each sheet with the tiniest glimmer of olive oil before folding in half lengthways. Brush the pastry with oil again.

6 With the pastry sheet stretched out in front of you, carefully place about 1 dessertspoon of mince at the bottom of the pastry sheet, closest to you. Very gingerly, bring the bottom corner of the pastry up to form the beginning of a triangle over the mince. Continue to fold the pastry into triangles until there is no more left and the mince is completely cocooned in a triangular filo parcel.

7 Place the finished triangle on a greased baking tray and brush the top with a little more oil. Continue folding the filo sheets until you have used up all the mince mixture.

8 Bake a preheated oven for 30 minutes, until golden.

**Makes:** approximately 18 samosas
**Prep time:** 45 minutes
**Cooking time:** 30 minutes

# mackerel salad with beetroot and horseradish dressing

Mackerel is cheap, very nutritious and quick to cook. This recipe is for fresh mackerel but I have cooked it with smoked mackerel fillets (which can be bought in any supermarket) and it has tasted delicious too. Beetroot can be bought ready-cooked but be careful not to buy the type doused in malt vinegar.

100g/4oz cooked beetroot
1 tbsp horseradish sauce
50ml/1¾fl oz half-fat crème fraîche
3 tbsp olive oil
salt and pepper
2 mackerel, filleted
oakleaf lettuce mixed with Swiss chard
    (or other similar reddish salad leaves)

1  Put the beetroot, horseradish and crème fraîche into the food processor and pulse until smooth. Add the olive oil and pulse again. Season with pepper and a little salt and put to one side.

2  Preheat the grill to hot.

3  Take the mackerel fillets and slash the skin side 3 or 4 times with a sharp knife. Lay on a lightly greased baking tray, skin side up. Put under the grill for 2–3 minutes until cooked through.

4  Arrange the salad leaves on 2 plates. Carefully place 2 fillets on top of each plate of salad before drizzling with the beetroot dressing. Serve with plenty of crusty brown bread.

**Serves:** 2
**Prep time:** 10 minutes
**Cooking time:** 2–3 minutes

# warm potato, chorizo and parsley salad

*The key to this salad is to treat the parsley as an equally important ingredient, rather than just a garnish. This also works wonderfully as part of a barbecue.*

600g/21oz new potatoes, cut into even-sized pieces
   weighing about 25g/1oz each
pinch of Maldon sea salt
250g/9oz chorizo
6 spring onions, sliced
½ lemon, juiced
150g/5oz flat-leaf parsley leaves, roughly chopped
freshly ground black pepper

1 Put the potatoes in a medium saucepan, cover with water and add a generous pinch of salt. Bring to the boil and simmer for 15–20 minutes until tender.

2 Peel the paper wrapping off the chorizo and slice into quarters lengthways. Now cut each piece into slices about ¼ cm/⅛ inch wide. Heat a non-stick frying pan until hot before adding the chorizo slices. Fry the chorizo until the fat starts to run and the edges begin to char.

3 When the potatoes are cooked, drain thoroughly before adding to the chorizo. Stir well.

4 Remove from the heat and add the sliced spring onions, lemon juice and chopped parsley. Stir to make sure the parsley and onions are evenly distributed throughout the salad. Season well with pepper.

5 Tip into a serving dish and serve with crusty bread.

**Serves** 4
**Prep time:** 15 minutes
**Cooking time:** 20 minutes

# Picnics and Treats

All children love eating outdoors, especially in the summer, though if mine had their own way they'd be picnicking outside in the middle of winter! For me the best thing about eating outdoors is that the grown-ups can sit down and be lazy whilst all the children run around as much as they like. Birthday parties work particularly well outdoors, I think. We had a really simple one for Megan this year and she said it was the best birthday she'd ever had. I was so touched! It just goes to show that you don't need to worry about devising really fancy outings or getting everything perfect.

All the recipes in this section are extremely portable and straightforward to prepare, which also makes them ideal for lunch boxes.

Iced tomato soup

Tarragon chicken

Crab cakes

Red rice salad with prawns and
sun-dried tomatoes

Chicken and mango salad

Honey and mustard sticky chicken

Broad bean, pancetta and goats'
cheese salad

Mango fruit crisps

Rhubarb tarts

Mini party cakes

Cinnamon apple turnovers

Fruit salad tubs

Fresh raspberry ice lollies

Toffee apples

Nutty chocolate balls

# iced tomato soup

*I think it was the fascination of the ice cube in this soup that got my children hooked on this! Perfect to have in a flask as a refreshing picnic treat.*

100g/4oz unsalted butter
500g/18oz onions, sliced
Maldon sea salt
black pepper
2kg/4½lb large tomatoes, cut into
  quarters and cored

170ml/6fl oz dry sherry
2 tbsp caster sugar
10 large fresh basil leaves
8 balls baby mozzarella (optional)
drizzle of olive oil
6–8 ice cubes

1 Melt the butter in a pan. Add the onions and a pinch of salt and some black pepper and cook till soft. Stir in the tomatoes, sherry and sugar.

2 Simmer for 40 minutes then add the basil and simmer for a further 20 minutes.

3 Blitz this all together in the food processor until smooth.

4 Sieve the soup back into the pan. Add water if necessary, season then allow to cool, then refrigerate for at least 1 hour.

5 Serve this soup (unless it is out of mugs) with a little extra basil, sliced baby mozzarella balls, a drizzle of olive oil and an ice cube. Finish with a twist of black pepper.

**Makes:** 6–8 mugs
**Prep time:** 20 minutes
**Cooking time:** 1 hour
**Chilling time:** 1½ hours

# tarragon chicken

*This wonderful summery dish always tastes better eaten in the garden with buttered new potatoes and a crisp salad full of fresh herbs. Your butcher will happily joint a chicken for you if you don't feel confident about doing it yourself. Alternatively, replace the chicken with a mixture of chicken breasts, thighs and drumsticks, readily available at the supermarket.*

1 medium chicken, jointed into 8 pieces
16 shallots, peeled
6 garlic cloves, peeled and thinly sliced
50ml/1¾fl oz tarragon vinegar
150ml/5fl oz vermouth (I use Noilly Prat)

½ quality chicken stock cube dissolved
   in 250ml/9fl oz water
100ml/4fl oz half-fat crème fraîche
25g/1oz bunch tarragon, leaves removed
   and roughly chopped

1 In a large lidded frying pan, brown the chicken on all sides in batches on a medium heat. Transfer to a plate.

2 Fry the shallots until they begin to colour. Add the garlic cloves and continue to fry until all are golden.

3 Increase the heat and add the tarragon vinegar and vermouth. Let it spit and bubble and reduce until about half the liquid remains.

4 Return the chicken to the pan.

5 Add the stock and bring to the boil. Reduce the heat to a simmer, cover with the lid and cook for 15 minutes.

6 Increase the heat a little and cook for a further 15 minutes without the lid.

7 Remove from the heat. Place the chicken pieces on a warm serving dish. Stir the crème fraîche and half the tarragon into the sauce. Pour the sauce over the chicken and sprinkle with the remaining chopped tarragon.

**Serves:** 4
**Prep time:** 15–20 minutes
**Cooking time:** 45 minutes

# crab cakes

Unlike most recipes for fish cakes, this doesn't contain any mashed potatoes. The texture is quite firm, making them an ideal picnic food that won't crumble if children are running about holding them.

200g/7oz tinned crab meat
200g/7oz skinned cod fillet
1 tbsp soy sauce
1 tsp fish sauce
4 spring onions, including green parts,
　roughly chopped

1 lime, zest and juice
1 garlic clove, crushed
25g/1oz bunch coriander, finely chopped
　including stalks
plain flour, for shaping
4 tbsp olive oil

1　Put all the ingredients, excluding the flour and olive oil, into a food processor and pulse until smooth.

2　Using well-floured hands and a well-floured surface, shape into 10 patties. Dust on all sides with flour.

3　Heat the olive oil in a frying pan and fry the patties for about 7 minutes on each side. When cooked, lay on kitchen paper until cool.

**Makes:** 10 crab cakes
**Prep time:** 15–20 minutes
**Cooking time:** 14 minutes

# red rice salad with prawns and sun-dried tomatoes

*Camargue red rice is absolutely delicious. Its slightly chewy texture and faint nutty flavour goes really well with the prawns and sun-dried tomatoes in this salad.*

225g/8oz Camargue red rice
340g/12oz prawns
10 sun-dried tomatoes
1 tbsp olive oil
salt and pepper

FOR THE DRESSING
5 tbsp olive oil
3 tbsp balsamic vinegar
juice of 1 lemon
1 tbsp wholegrain mustard

1 Bring to the boil a pan of water seasoned with a couple of pinches of salt. Add the rice and cook as directed.

2 Shell the prawns and put to one side.

3 Make the dressing by mixing together the oil, vinegar, lemon juice and mustard in a small bowl.

4 Slice the sun-dried tomatoes and mix together with the prawns. Drain the rice and run under cold water to refresh it.

5 In a large frying pan, heat the oil, add the rice, prawns and sun-dried tomatoes and fry for 2–3 minutes. Pour over the dressing and carefully stir through. Season as necessary.

6 Serve either warm or at room temperature.

**Serves:** 4 as part of a selection of salads
**Prep time:** 10 minutes
**Cooking time:** 20 minutes

# chicken and mango salad

*A really light and fresh salad — like the taste, the colours are amazingly vibrant.*

2 chicken breasts
4 tbsp olive oil
1 mango
2 red chilli peppers, deseeded and
  finely chopped
3 spring onions, finely sliced

juice of 2 limes
1 little gem lettuce, cut into strips
handful of rocket leaves
3 tbsp balsamic vinegar
1 tbsp coriander,
  finely chopped

1  Drizzle the chicken breasts with 2 tbsp olive oil and grill under a moderate heat until cooked. Leave to cool.

2  Peel the mango, cut into 2cm/¾ inch cubes and place in a bowl with the chilli peppers and spring onions. Squeeze over the lime juice and mix gently, being careful not to squash the mango.

3  In another bowl, gently toss the little gem lettuce and rocket leaves with the balsamic vinegar and 2 tbsp of olive oil, ensuring all is covered. Transfer to a large, clean bowl.

4  Cut the chicken into chunks and carefully combine with the mango mixture. Add the coriander and mix through gently, then transfer to the prepared salad bowl.

**Serves:** 4–6 as a picnic salad
**Prep time:** 15 minutes
**Cooking time:** 15–20 minutes (plus time to cool)

# honey and mustard sticky chicken

*Chicken pieces are the quintessential picnic food – easy to carry, easy to eat, messy and sticky. Everybody eats them so you can never do enough…*

12 chicken drumsticks (skin on)
12 chicken thighs (skin on)

FOR THE MARINADE
4 tbsp runny honey
4 tbsp wholegrain mustard
zest and juice of 2 lemons
4 tbsp soy sauce

1  Preheat the oven to 190°C/375°F/GM5.

2  Place the marinade ingredients into a small pan and stir gently over a low heat. This melts the honey and makes it easier to pour over the chicken.

3  Place the chicken pieces on lightly greased oven trays. Pour over the marinade, ensuring all pieces are generously covered.

4  Place in the oven and roast for 30–35 minutes. Turn the chicken over from time to time and keep rolling it in the marinade in the bottom of the oven trays until the meat is golden brown.

**Serves:** 12
**Prep time:** 15 minutes
**Cooking time:** 30–35 minutes

TIP

■  These are great served warm or cold.

# broad bean, pancetta and goats' cheese salad

4 tbsp olive oil
200g/7oz chèvre goats' cheese, halved
200g/7oz cubed pancetta
2 garlic cloves, finely chopped
300g/10oz frozen broad beans in their pods,
   blanched and refreshed, shells removed
juice of ½ lemon
handful of chopped mint

1  Put the frozen broad beans into a bowl of water and set aside.

2  Heat 2 tbsp of olive oil in a grill pan and add the goats' cheese. Make sure the cheese is covered with oil and grill for 1½ minutes on each side until lightly golden.

3  Fry the pancetta in a frying pan for 2 minutes and add the chopped garlic. Cook for a further minute then add the broad beans and lemon juice. Cook this together for a further minute or two.

4  Transfer the salad to the centre of a plate, dividing into four portions and placing the goats' cheese on top. Sprinkle over the fresh mint and drizzle with remaining olive oil.

**Serves:** 4 as part of selection of salads
**Prep time:** 15 minutes
**Cooking time:** 10–15 minutes

# mango fruit crisps

*Dried fruit is always a good treat. It has enough natural sugar to give children a little natural pick-me-up in the afternoon before activities, or even to keep smaller ones awake till bedtime! A great alternative to a snack bar and not too messy.*

**1 large mango (fairly ripe)**

1  Preheat the oven to 90°C/195°F/GM¼.

2  Peel the skin off the mango then slice off the cheeks (the soft flesh), leaving the core in a square chunk. Discard the core.

3  Slice the cheeks very thinly. Lay these slices on some greaseproof paper on an oven tray.

4  Place in the oven for approximately ½ hour, then turn the slices over and put back in the oven for a further ½ hour. The slices should have almost dried out but not be too crispy.

5  Remove from the oven and allow them to air-dry for a further ½ hour.

6  The slices should be dried but still have a slightly chewy texture.

**Makes:** approx 16 slices depending on the size of the mango
**Prep time:** 10 minutes
**Cooking/air-drying time:** 1½ hours – the longer the better

## TIPS

■  This is delicious done with apple as well. Simply slice the apple (don't peel it) around the width as thinly as you can and follow the same cooking instructions as for the mango.

■  Both mango and apple slices are best stored in food bags, and will last at least a couple of days.

# rhubarb tarts

The quantities for the jam make more than enough for 24 jam tarts. It's so simple to make and tastes so good on hot buttered toast that it seems silly not to make a little extra. For the patterns on top of the tarts, I use small pastry cutters in the shapes of hearts and stars.

FOR THE JAM
750g/26oz fresh rhubarb
300g/10½oz caster sugar
100ml/4fl oz water
1 vanilla pod split lengthways, seeds removed

450g/1lb pack ready-rolled shortcrust pastry
2 tbsp milk

1 To make the jam, cut the rhubarb into 1cm/½ inch chunks and put in a medium saucepan along with the sugar, water, vanilla seeds and pod. Bring to the boil, reduce the heat to the lowest setting and put on the lid. Cook for 10 minutes until the sugar has dissolved.

2 Take off the lid, increase the heat until you have a steady, rolling boil and continue to cook for a further 30 minutes. Remove from the heat and allow to cool.

3 Preheat the oven to 180°F/350°F/GM4.

4 Grease two 12-hole mince pie tins and roll out the pastry onto a well-floured surface. Using a rolling pin, flatten the pastry out. Cut out 24 circles of pastry with a crinkled pastry cutter (about 8cm/3 inches in diameter) and gently push down into the tart moulds.

5 Put a dessertspoon of jam into each pastry case.

6 Using smaller pastry cutters, cut out 24 stars and hearts and lightly brush with a little milk. Place a shape on top of each dollop of jam.

7 Put in the oven and cook for 20 minutes. Remove and leave in the tins for 10 minutes before placing on a wire rack.

Makes: 24 tarts
Prep time: 30 minutes
Cooking time: 50 minutes

# mini party cakes

*I love making fairy cakes – they're always a guaranteed hit. I sometimes prefer them to one big birthday cake as it's so much easier handing them out than slicing up a huge cake and wondering if you'll have enough. Even better, no one can accuse you of dealing out unequal portions!*

250g/9oz unsalted butter, softened
250g/9oz caster sugar
4 eggs
250g/9oz self-raising flour

FOR THE BUTTER ICING
225g/8oz butter, softened
450g/1lb icing sugar
splash of milk or water
food colouring (optional)
hundreds and thousands to decorate (optional)

1 Preheat the oven to 180°C/350°F/GM4 and line two 12-hole muffin tins with paper cases (if you only have 1 tin you can make the cakes in 2 batches).

2 Beat together the butter and sugar until pale and fluffy, then beat in the eggs 1 at a time.

3 Fold in the sieved flour and mix together well.

4 Spoon the mixture into the paper cases then bake in the oven for 15–20 minutes until golden brown. The sponge should rise to the touch.

5 Remove the cakes from the tins and set aside on a cooling rack.

6 To make the icing, put the butter and icing sugar in a bowl, adding a splash of milk or water and a couple of drops of food colouring if desired. Beat together until smooth.

7 When cool, decorate the mini sponges with the butter icing and a sprinkle of hundreds and thousands, if desired.

**Makes:** 24 mini cakes
**Prep time:** 15 minutes
**Cooking time:** 15–20 minutes

TIP

■ For a citrus twist, add the zest of a lemon or orange to the sponge mixture and a squeeze of the juice to the butter icing instead of the milk.

# cinnamon apple turnovers

*Apple turnovers make the perfect pudding for a summer picnic. When the children have had enough of keeping still and the adults want to relax and chat, an apple turnover can be thrust into a child's hand and they can eat their pudding running about in the sunshine. Alternatively, serve on plates with clotted cream on the side.*

6 apples (3 Cox and 3 Granny Smith),
 peeled, cored and finely sliced
½ tsp ground cinnamon
½ lemon, juiced
100g/4oz currants

25g/1oz soft brown sugar
425g/15oz pack ready-rolled puff
 pastry
50ml/1¾fl oz milk
2 tbsp demerara sugar

1  Put the sliced apple, ground cinnamon, lemon juice, currants and soft brown sugar into a large saucepan and put on a medium heat. Stir well to make sure the sugar and spices are evenly spread over the apple. Cook for about 5 minutes then remove from the heat, put the lid on the saucepan and allow to cool.

2  Put the sheets of pastry on a well-floured surface and roll out to make each sheet 15cm/ 6 inches square. Cut each sheet into 4 squares.

3  Preheat the oven to 190°C/375°F/GM5

4  Divide the apple mixture between the 8 pastry squares, spooning the mixture into the centre of each one. Using a pastry brush, lightly brush the edge of the pastry with a little milk before folding each square in half diagonally to make a triangle. Crimp the edges together to seal in the apple.

5  Brush each pastry case with a little milk and make a couple of small slashes in the top with a sharp knife. Finally, sprinkle with a little demerara sugar.

6  Place on a baking sheet lined with greaseproof paper and cook in the oven for 20 minutes until golden. Remove to a wire rack to cool.

**Makes:** 8
**Prep time:** 30 minutes
**Cooking time:** 25 minutes

# fruit salad tubs

*You can use any combination of fruit you like for this recipe. I tend to choose what looks good when I go shopping.*

¼ watermelon, deseeded, peeled and
    cut into 2½ cm/1 inch pieces
1 mango, peeled and cut into 2½ cm/
    1 inch pieces
½ cantaloupe melon, deseeded, peeled
    and cut into 2½ cm/1 inch pieces

2 kiwi fruits, peeled and sliced
white grapes, sliced in half
12 cherries, halved and stoned
275ml/10fl oz apple juice
2½ cm/1 inch piece ginger, peeled and
    roughly chopped

1   Prepare all the fruit and place gently into a large mixing bowl, taking care not to squash the pieces.

2   In a small saucepan, gently heat the apple juice and ginger for approximately 5 minutes.

3   Remove from the heat and allow to cool completely.

4   Sieve out the ginger.

5   To serve, pour the apple juice over the fruit salad and divide between 8 4–6 oz individual tubs.

**Makes:** 8 small tubs
**Prep time:** 20 minutes (if you chop slowly like me...)
**Cooking time:** 5 minutes (to heat apple juice and ginger)

TIP

- If you have young children joining you, cut the fruit into smaller pieces – especially grapes and cherries – to avoid the danger of choking.

# fresh raspberry ice lollies

*Never wear your best clothes with these – they stain! A great treat for a summer's day.*

200g/7oz caster sugar
250ml/9fl oz water
450g/1lb fresh raspberries
12 wooden lolly sticks

1 Put the sugar and water into a pan and stir over a moderate heat until the sugar has dissolved. Bring to the boil then remove from the heat and allow to cool.

2 Pop the raspberries into the liquidizer and whiz till smooth, then mix together with the cooled sugar syrup.

3 Pour the mixture into lolly moulds and place in the freezer.

4 Freeze for approximately 2½ hours then add the lolly sticks. Wooden sticks are the nicest – simply push them into the bottom of the lolly then return to the freezer and allow to freeze overnight.

5 Remove when ready to serve. It's best to take them out of the freezer 10 minutes before so it's easy to remove them from the moulds.

**Makes:** approximately 12 lollies
**Prep time:** 15 minutes
**Freezing time:** 2½ hours

TIP

■ Strawberries make great lollies too. Just pop them in the liquidizer.

# toffee apples

I know these are terrible for kids' teeth but everyone is allowed something really naughty at times! These are the ultimate in picnic treats.

450g/1lb demerara sugar
225ml/8fl oz water
1 tsp malt vinegar
4 tbsp golden syrup
50g/2oz butter
12 wooden lolly sticks
12 Golden Delicious apples (or similar)
12 squares of cellophane paper, optional
ribbon, optional

1 Dissolve the sugar in the water over a moderate heat. When it has all dissolved (approximately 10 minutes), stir in the vinegar, syrup and butter, then bring to the boil. Let it bubble fairly gently for around 15–20 minutes until it resembles a treacly syrup. A good way to test if it is ready is to drop a little into a bowl of water – if ready, it will form a hard ball.

2 Meanwhile, push the lolly sticks firmly into the base of the apples.

3 Dip each apple in turn into the hot toffee, turning to ensure it is evenly coated, then place top side down onto a lightly greased tray to cool and set.

4 Once set – and if you are not eating them straight away – you can wrap your toffee apples with brightly coloured cellophane and tie with a ribbon (if you want to be fancy!).

**Makes:** 12
**Prep time:** 15 minutes
**Cooking time:** 30 minutes

TIP

■ Please remind children not to bite too hard!

# nutty chocolate balls

*Naughty, but nice!*

100g/4oz white chocolate
100g/4oz milk chocolate plus
   2 tbsp double cream
170g/6oz mix of pistachio/macadamia
   and hazelnuts, crushed roughly with
   a pestle and mortar

1  Melt both chocolates (the milk chocolate with the double cream added) in separate bowls over boiling water until runny and smooth.

2  Divide the crushed nuts between the two bowls of chocolate and stir in well until coated.

3  Cut out approximately 15–20 squares of clingfilm and lay on a surface. Spoon around 1 tbsp of the chocolate nut mix onto each square, then shape into a ball and twist the top of the clingfilm to hold the shape.

4  Place on a tray or plate and put in the fridge to set. This will take at least 2 hours.

5  Remove from the fridge, take off the clingfilm and serve.

**Makes:** 15–20, depending on size
**Prep time:** 20 minutes
**Setting time:** 2 hours

# Food in a Flash

During the week I often don't have the time or energy to make food in advance – a glass of wine after the kids have gone to bed is usually more appealing than going back into the kitchen to make tomorrow's tea! This means I'm often under pressure to cook dinner from scratch in a few minutes.

The recipes in this section are some of my favourite fall-backs. They're quick, they're easy and always go down a treat.

Chicken escalopes with green pepper salad

Asparagus and prawn risotto

Pasta with mushrooms and bacon

Salmon and vegetables en papillote

Veal parmesan

Grandma's bones

Nectarines marinated in honey and ginger

Raspberries with orange

# chicken escalopes with green pepper salad

This wonderful weeknight summer supper is very quick to make. If the radishes are out of season, substitute with half a finely chopped red onion.

FOR THE SALAD
1 green pepper, cut into dice no more
  than 1cm/½ inch square
1 red chilli, deseeded and finely sliced
10 radishes, diced
6 spring onions, sliced (including part
  of the green stalk)
2 limes, juiced
4 tbsp olive oil
small bunch of coriander leaves, chopped

FOR THE CHICKEN
2 chicken breasts
6 tbsp breadcrumbs
½ tsp cayenne pepper
½ tsp paprika
½ tsp celery salt
pepper
1 egg, beaten
olive oil for frying

1 Make the salad first by combining all the ingredients except the coriander. Set aside. The red from the radishes will run into the lime juice and colour the salad in a pretty way.

2 Carefully slice the chicken breasts horizontally, trying to get them about ¾ cm/⅓ inch thick. The sharper the knife, the easier it will be.

3 Mix together the breadcrumbs, spices and pepper. Put the breadcrumb mixture into a shallow, wide bowl, such as a soup plate.

4 Put the beaten egg into a similar bowl and dunk each sliver of chicken in the egg. Place the chicken in the breadcrumbs and turn it over until evenly coated. Place on a clean plate and continue until all the chicken pieces are thoroughly covered with breadcrumbs.

5 Heat a frying pan until hot. Add about 2 tbsp olive oil and fry the chicken pieces for 2 minutes each side until golden. You may need to add olive oil between batches.

6 Just before serving, stir in the chopped coriander to the green pepper salad. Serve with warm French bread to soak up the limey salad dressing.

Serves: 2
Prep time: 10–15 minutes
Cooking time: 5 minutes

# asparagus and prawn risotto

*Risotto is quick and easy to make and one of the most comforting meals I know.*

200g/7oz king prawns, precooked and shelled
1 litre/1¾ pints chicken stock (in emergencies this can be made with 2 quality chicken stock cubes and 1 litre/1¾ pints water)
100g/4oz unsalted butter
2 onions, finely chopped

1 garlic clove, crushed
250g/9oz pack fresh asparagus spears cut to about 10cm/4 inches long. Slice into 1cm/½ inch pieces, but separate the tips of the asparagus from the slices of stalk.
225g/8oz arborio rice
200ml/7fl oz white wine
50g/2oz Parmesan, grated

1 Before you start to cook, take the prawns out of the fridge and tip onto a plate to allow them to come up to room temperature.

2 Put the stock in a saucepan and bring to the boil. Reduce the heat to a very low simmer.

3 Melt the butter in a large sauté pan and add the onions and garlic. Cook for 5 minutes until the onions have softened but not coloured.

4 Add the sliced pieces of asparagus stalk (not the tips) and cook for about 1 minute before adding the rice. Stir until the grains start to soften.

5 Pour over the wine and increase the heat until the wine has all but disappeared.

6 Reduce the heat and begin adding the hot stock, a ladle at a time. It is important that you let the rice absorb all the stock before adding any more. If you drench the rice with stock, the end result will be more like slops than risotto. Continue to add the stock gradually, stirring the bubbling pan at all times.

7 When you have about 2 ladles of stock left, throw in the asparagus tips and the prawns. Stir well and add the remaining stock.

8 Finally, stir in the grated Parmesan and serve immediately on warm plates with a little extra Parmesan sprinkled on top.

**Serves:** 4
**Prep time:** 10 minutes
**Cooking time:** 20 minutes

# pasta with mushrooms and bacon

*This is real emergency comfort food and it takes only minutes to prepare. Serve with lots of watercress to offset the richness of the sauce.*

2 tbsp olive oil
200g/7oz unsmoked streaky bacon,
    thinly sliced
1 medium onion, finely chopped
1 garlic clove, crushed
250g/9oz mushrooms, sliced

100ml/4fl oz white wine
100g/4oz dry spaghetti per person
200ml/7fl oz single cream
25g/1oz flat-leaf parsley, finely
    chopped
grated Parmesan, to serve

1  In a medium frying pan, heat the olive oil before adding the bacon. Fry on a medium heat until the fat starts to run.

2  Add the chopped onion and garlic and continue frying until the onion starts to colour.

3  Meanwhile, put a large saucepan of salted water on to boil.

4  Stir the mushrooms into the bacon and onion until they start to flop. Add the wine and increase the heat until it has almost evaporated.

5  Put the spaghetti into the pan of boiling water and stir well. Bring to the boil, stirring all the time. Reduce the heat a little and allow to cook according to the instructions on the packet.

6  Add the cream to the bacon and mushroom mixture and return to a very gentle simmer for 3–4 minutes.

7  When the spaghetti is cooked, drain and return to the pan. Pour over the sauce and stir in the chopped parsley.

8  Divide between bowls and serve with freshly grated Parmesan.

**Serves:** 3 (or 2 if very, very hungry)
**Prep time:** 10 minutes
**Cooking time:** 20 minutes

# salmon and vegetables en papillote

*This method of cooking fish is so easy and the children love it, especially when they have their own little fish parcels. The steaming process traps all the goodness and flavour of the fish – what could be better?!*

4 tbsp olive oil
4 salmon fillets
2 garlic cloves, thinly sliced
1 red chilli, deseeded and finely
   chopped
1 large shallot, peeled and thinly sliced

1 carrot, peeled and cut into thin matchsticks
8 sugar snap peas, halved lengthways
8 stems of purple sprouting broccoli
16 green olives
1 tbsp chopped flat-leaf parsley
salt and pepper

1 Preheat the oven to 190°C/375°F/GM5.

2 Take 4 squares of greaseproof paper, measuring approximately 23cm/9 inches square. Drizzle with a little of the olive oil and sit the salmon fillets on top.

3 Sprinkle over the garlic, chilli and shallot and arrange the remaining ingredients on top. Season with a little salt and pepper.

4 Wrap up the paper to form a parcel, folding the edges to seal it. Place on a baking sheet and bake for 10–15 minutes.

**Serves:** 4
**Prep time:** 15–20 minutes
**Cooking time:** 15–20 minutes

# veal parmesan

*A firm favourite of Holly's – she requests this at least once a month!*
*You can also prepare this the night before. Refrigerating the steaks overnight*
*helps the breadcrumbs stick when you grill the steaks.*

6 veal steaks (about 1cm/½ inch thick)
3 garlic cloves
3 eggs, beaten
12 tbsp breadcrumbs
small bunch of fresh parsley, finely
   chopped
salt and pepper
50g/2oz Parmesan cheese, grated
300g/10½oz spaghetti
3 tbsp olive oil

FOR THE TOMATO SAUCE
2 tbsp olive oil
2 small onions, finely chopped
1 clove garlic, crushed
1 chilli, deseeded and finely chopped
2 packs vine cherry tomatoes, halved
2 tbsp Worcester sauce
1 tbsp soy sauce
salt and pepper
handful of fresh basil, roughly torn

1  Start with your steaks. Crush the garlic and rub it on both sides of each steak. Place the beaten eggs in a shallow bowl. In a separate bowl, mix the breadcrumbs with the parsley, seasoning and Parmesan. Dip each piece of steak in the egg mix then into the breadcrumbs, ensuring each side is well coated. Lay the steaks on a large plate, cover with clingfilm and refrigerate for a couple of hours.

2  To make the sauce, heat your oil in a medium pan then add the onions, garlic and chilli. Let them soften then add the tomatoes. Stir together then leave the tomatoes to break down. Add the Worcester and soy sauces, a good grinding of black pepper and a pinch of salt, and toss in the basil leaves. Let this sauce simmer gently for 20–25 minutes. I like to blitz the sauce in the liquidizer and serve it smooth, but you may prefer to leave it as it is.

3  Put a pan of water on to boil. When the water is boiling, add the pasta, a pinch of salt and a dash of oil. Cook as directed on your packet.

4  Heat the grill to 240°C/475°F/GM9. Drizzle a little olive oil over both sides of each steak. Place under the grill for 5–10 minutes each side until golden and slightly sizzling.

5  Serve 1 steak per plate with a portion of pasta and a generous serving of sauce. Sprinkle some more fresh parsley over the top.

**Serves:** 6
**Prep time:** 15 minutes
**Cooking time:** 20–25 minutes for the sauce and 10–20 minutes to grill the steaks

# grandma's bones

This recipe isn't as sinister as it sounds! My mum always cooks spare ribs for the children in this way, and this is what the children have ended up calling them.

**16 spare ribs, separated**
**Worcester sauce (approximately 3 tbsp)**
**dark soy sauce (approximately 6 tbsp)**

1 Preheat the oven to 200°C/400°F/GM6.

2 Place the ribs onto a lightly greased oven tray, sprinkle over the Worcester sauce followed by a slightly more generous amount of soy sauce.

3 Roast in the oven for approximately 15–20 minutes.

**Serves:** 4 each for 4 children
**Prep time:** 5 minutes
**Cooking time:** 15–20 minutes

# nectarines marinated in honey and ginger

4 nectarines, each sliced into 8 wedges
8 wooden skewers
3 tbsp runny clear honey
2½ cm/1 inch piece ginger, grated

1 Thread the nectarine wedges onto 8 wooden skewers and place on a tray.

2 Put the honey and ginger in a small saucepan and heat gently for 2–3 minutes.

3 Tip the honey and ginger marinade over the nectarine wedges. Cover with clingfilm and leave to marinate for at least ½ hour at room temperature.

4 When you are ready to serve, place the skewers either on the barbecue or under the grill for a couple of minutes each side.

**Makes:** 8 skewers
**Prep time:** 10 minutes (plus ½ hour to marinate)
**Cooking time:** 4 minutes

TIP

- Vanilla ice cream makes a great accompaniment.

# raspberries with orange

*This fantastic emergency pudding takes just minutes to prepare and tastes fresh and delicious. Serve with vanilla ice cream or crème fraîche.*

500g/18oz fresh raspberries
6 oranges, juiced
5 generous sprigs of mint, thinly sliced

1 Put the raspberries into a serving bowl and set aside.

2 Pour the orange juice into a saucepan and bring to the boil. Let it boil furiously until it has halved in quantity. Allow to cool.

3 When the juice is at room temperature, or just above if you're in a hurry, sprinkle the raspberries with the mint and pour over the orange juice. Stir lightly to distribute the mint throughout the raspberries.

Serves: 4
Prep time: 1 minute
Cooking time: 5–7 minutes
Cooling time: 5 minutes

TIP

■ If you're really short on time, simply use 300ml/11fl oz of fresh orange juice.

# Try Something Different

There is nothing more important to me than getting the children to be a little adventurous in what they eat. If we all go out to dinner together I want them to be able to order off the same menus as Gordon and me and not make a fuss about having a special children's menu.

The recipes in this section work well as little first courses or snacks to share. My children feel really grown up when they think they are having a starter and it's also a fantastic way of introducing them to different flavours. Don't feel you have to follow up an Asian-style dish with a similar-themed main course. The point is to introduce new flavours alongside tastes your children are familiar with and not make a big deal of it.

Calamari fritti

Roasted garlic and lime aioli

Crab and sweetcorn soup

Sesame prawn toast

Bang bang chicken

Chinese chicken wings

Chilli beef stir-fry

Sweet and sour pork

Thai-ish chicken soup

Butter chicken

Sausages with lentils

Minced lamb curry

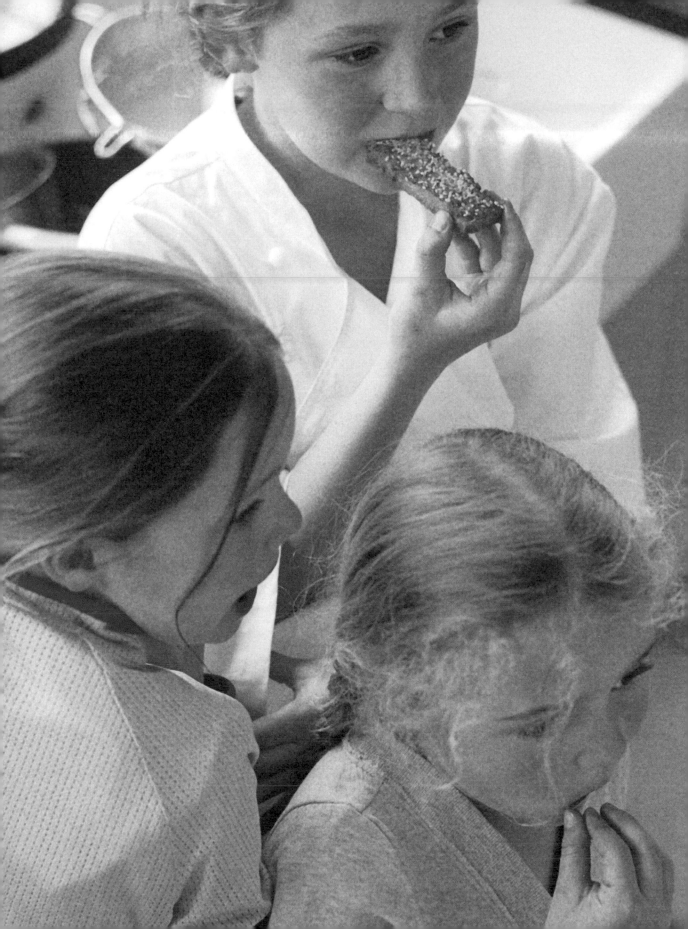

# calamari fritti

*Fun finger food for all the family to enjoy – a tasty alternative to popcorn in front of a DVD.*

450g/1lb squid (fresh or frozen)
oil for deep-frying (enough to a have
   depth of 2½ cm/1 inch in the pan)
170g/6oz plain flour
1 tsp paprika

1 tsp cayenne pepper
1 lemon, sliced
pinch of salt
roasted garlic and lime aioli
   (see page 100)

1 Cut the squid into rings approximately 1cm/½ inch thick. Clean if necessary or, if frozen, make sure it is thoroughly defrosted.

2 Pour oil in a pan to a depth of approximately 2½ cm/1 inch. Heat the oil until just beginning to smoke.

3 While the oil is heating, mix together the flour, paprika and cayenne pepper in a large bowl. Add the squid rings and make sure all are covered.

4 When the oil is ready, remove a couple of the rings (it's best to do this in batches), shake off the excess flour and lower into the oil. Fry until golden, remove from the oil and place on kitchen roll to absorb the excess. Continue until all are done.

5 Serve while warm with slices of lemon, a sprinkle of salt and the roasted garlic and lime aioli (page 100).

**Serves:** 6 as a starter or snack
**Prep time:** 15 minutes
**Cooking time:** 3–4 minutes

# roasted garlic and lime aioli

This recipe makes enough to go with the calamari on page 99. It's also fantastic served with chunky chips, bruschetta, fish cakes or any white fish. It will keep in the fridge for up to three days.

2 bulbs of garlic
2 tsp olive oil
8 tbsp mayonnaise
1 tsp lemon rind
2 tbsp lime juice
1 tsp salt
¼ tsp Tabasco (optional)

1 Preheat the oven to 220°C/425°F/GM7.

2 Peel off the outside layers of the garlic bulbs, taking care to leave the cores in place to keep the cloves together. Cut off and discard the top quarter of each bulb, place them cut side up in the centre of a piece of tin foil and drizzle over the olive oil. Fold the foil around them tightly and bake for approximately 45 minutes, until the garlic is soft.

3 Remove and allow to cool. Discard all the skins and scoop out the soft pulp. Mash until smooth with the rest of the ingredients.

4 Place in the fridge to cool completely.

**Prep time:** 15 minutes
**Cooking time:** 45 minutes
**Chilling time:** at least 20 minutes

# crab and sweetcorn soup

This is a brilliant lunchtime soup which gently introduces children to a Chinese classic and crab all at once. I rarely specify using fresh stock in recipes because, quite simply, it is easier to use water and a stock cube. However, in this recipe the quality of the stock is key to the flavour of the final soup, so I do think it's essential to use either a homemade chicken stock or a very good-quality bought stock.

1 egg white
1 tsp sesame oil
1.2 litres/2 pints homemade or good-quality bought chicken stock
300g/10½oz frozen sweetcorn
1 tbsp dry sherry
1 tbsp soy sauce

5cm/2 inch piece fresh ginger, peeled and finely chopped
1 tsp sugar
2 tsp cornflour mixed with 1 tbsp water
250g/9oz fresh white crabmeat
salt and pepper as needed
5 spring onions, finely chopped, to garnish

1  In a small jug, mix together the egg white and sesame oil.

2  In a large saucepan, bring the stock to the boil and add the sweetcorn.

3  Add the sherry, soy sauce, ginger and sugar and simmer for 5 minutes. Slowly pour in the cornflour mixture and bring back to the boil, stirring all the time.

4  Add the crabmeat, immediately followed by the egg white mixture, carefully pouring it in with one hand while continuing to stir with the other.

5  Bring back to the boil, check seasoning and serve immediately, garnished with the chopped spring onions.

**Serves:** 4
**Prep time:** 10 minutes
**Cooking time:** 10 minutes

# sesame prawn toast

10 slices of white sliced bread
    (a little stale is best)
3 tbsp sesame seeds
groundnut oil for deep-frying the
    toasts (enough to have depth of
    2½ cm/1 inch in the pan)
soy sauce or sweet chilli sauce, to
    serve

FOR THE PRAWN PASTE
75g/3oz tinned water chestnuts
450g/1lb uncooked prawns, peeled
    and finely chopped
1 tsp salt
1 egg white
1 tbsp finely chopped ginger
2 tsp soy sauce
2 tsp sesame oil
2 tsp sugar

1  Mix together all the ingredients for the prawn paste. You can either finely chop it all or put it in the food processor until it is of a spreading consistency.

2  Cut the crusts off the bread and cut into rectangles of approximately 8 x 2½ cm/3 x 1 inches.

3  Spread the prawn paste on each piece of bread at a thickness of approximately 3mm/⅛ inch. Sprinkle sesame seeds over all the pieces.

4  Heat the groundnut oil in a pan until it is just beginning to smoke. Deep-fry the bread in batches, paste side down, for 2–3 minutes until golden, then turn over and repeat.

5  Remove with a slotted spoon and place onto kitchen roll to blot up the excess oil.

6  Serve while warm with a little soy or sweet chilli sauce on the side.

**Makes:** approximately 30 pieces
**Prep time:** 20 minutes
**Cooking time:** Approximately 6 minutes, until golden, per batch (about 24 minutes in total)

# bang bang chicken

My children first had this when we ventured out for a family Chinese, and after the initial excitement of chopsticks they resorted to using fingers or forks as this dish was too delicious to mess around with. I've tried several versions but this one is by far the best.

250g/9oz smooth peanut butter (or crunchy if preferred)
2 tbsp water
2 tbsp sweet chilli sauce
2 tbsp toasted sesame oil
1 tsp vegetable oil
3 skinless and boneless cooked chicken breasts
2 medium carrots, peeled and cut into long shreds
3 spring onions, cut into long shreds
½ cucumber, deseeded and cut into long shreds
2 tbsp rice vinegar
4 tsp sesame seeds, lightly toasted

1  Spoon the peanut butter into a bowl, add the water and stir through. Place over a pan of boiling water. When it starts to soften, add the chilli sauce and both oils and continue to mix through till it is of a pouring consistency.

2  Cut the chicken breasts into shreds and place to one side.

3  Put all the vegetables in a bowl and stir through the rice vinegar. Arrange on a serving plate, put the shredded chicken on top and spoon over the peanut sauce. Finish by sprinkling over the sesame seeds.

**Makes:** enough for 4 children as a starter
**Prep time:** 20 minutes
**Cooking time:** 10 minutes to soften the peanut butter

TIP

■  If you can find them, use smoked chicken breasts.

# chinese chicken wings

*Sticky, messy and delicious, just how they should be...*

900g/2lb chicken wings

FOR THE MARINADE
2 tbsp hoi sin sauce
2 tbsp soy sauce
4 tbsp tomato ketchup
1 clove garlic, crushed
1 tbsp runny honey
1 tbsp brown sugar
1 tbsp apple cider vinegar

1 Mix together all the marinade ingredients in a large bowl then add the chicken wings, ensuring they are well covered. Cover the bowl with clingfilm and place in the fridge for at least a couple of hours, preferably overnight.

2 When you are ready to cook the chicken, preheat the oven to 190°C/375°F/GM5.

3 Place the chicken wings on a lightly greased baking tray and place in the oven for 20–25 minutes. Brush on any excess marinade approximately halfway through the cooking time.

4 Check the chicken is thoroughly cooked and serve.

**Makes:** ough for 4 hungry children
**Prep time:** 15 minutes
**Marinating time:** 2 hours or overnight
**Cooking time:** 20–25 minutes

# chilli beef stir-fry

*This has to be one of the easiest and quickest dishes I know. Serve with noodles for a super-quick supper, or steamed rice if you're thinking slightly further ahead.*

600g/21oz rump steak
5 tbsp sweet chilli sauce
2 tbsp soy sauce
2 tbsp water
2 tbsp sesame oil
150g/5oz sugar snaps
6 spring onions, finely cut
100g/4oz cashew nuts

1  To cut the steak thinly and easily, slice it straight from the fridge. Try and cut it into slices about ½ cm/¼ inch wide.

2  In a small bowl, mix together the sweet chilli sauce, soy sauce and water.

3  Heat the sesame oil in a wok until it just begins to smoke. Add the beef, being very careful of the spitting fat, and stir-fry for 2–3 minutes until the beef browns.

4  Add the sugar snaps and cook for a further minute before adding the sweet chilli sauce mixture.

5  Bring it back to the boil, stirring constantly, and allow to bubble for no more than 2 minutes before adding the spring onions and cashew nuts.

6  Give it all one final, thorough stir before serving with the rice or noodles.

**Serves:** 4 children or 2–3 adults
**Prep time:** 10–15 minutes
**Cooking time:** 15 minutes

# sweet and sour pork

*A gentle introduction to the contrasting tastes of sweet and sour, this dish is so colourful with the different vegetables and always looks appealing to kids.*

3 tbsp groundnut oil
3 tbsp toasted sesame oil
2 small onions, finely chopped
2 cloves garlic, finely chopped
pinch of salt
340g/12oz diced pork
2 tsp Chinese five spice
1 red pepper, deseeded and sliced
1 yellow pepper, deseeded and sliced

1 courgette, halved lengthways and
   sliced horizontally
3 tbsp soy sauce
2 tbsp malt vinegar (or to taste)
1 tbsp soft brown sugar
3 tbsp sweetcorn
1 tin pineapple (227g/8oz) with juice
salt and pepper, to season
white rice, to serve

1 Heat the oils together in a large flat pan or wok. Add the onions and garlic and a pinch of salt and fry together until soft. Add the diced pork and allow to colour. Sprinkle in the five spice, add the peppers and courgette and stir-fry all together for a couple of minutes.

2 Add the soy sauce, vinegar, brown sugar and sweetcorn.

3 Cut the pineapple into chunks and add to the pan along with the juice.

4 Season to taste. To get the right balance of sweet and sour, adjust the vinegar and sugar quantities to your personal taste.

5 Allow the sauce to simmer over a low heat for approximately 40 minutes. If necessary, add a little water or stock.

6 Serve with white rice, cooked as directed on the packet.

**Serves:** 4 children
**Prep time:** 20 minutes
**Cooking time:** 40 minutes

TIP

- This tastes even better the next day, so it's a great one to make in advance.

# thai-ish chicken soup

This isn't in any way authentically Thai, but it does taste extremely good! If you're cooking this for children, reduce the amount of Thai green curry paste and leave out the red chilli. For a more adult twist, garnish with some finely chopped red chilli.

2 tbsp grape seed oil
1 tbsp Thai green curry paste
2½ cm/1 inch fresh ginger, chopped into
   small matchsticks
400ml/14fl oz coconut milk
500ml/18fl oz chicken stock (or 500ml/18fl
   oz water mixed with 1 chicken stock
   cube)
1 tbsp fish sauce

2 chicken breasts, thinly sliced
150g/5oz dry, medium noodles
100g/4oz green beans, halved
1 large carrot, cut into matchsticks
25g/1oz fresh coriander, chopped
6 spring onions, thinly sliced
1 red chilli, halved, deseeded and thinly
   chopped (optional)
1 lime, quartered, to serve

1  In a large saucepan, heat the grape seed oil before adding the Thai green curry paste. Cook gently for no more than a minute before adding the chopped ginger.

2  Gently pour on the coconut milk, chicken stock and fish sauce. Bring to the boil and simmer for a minute. Then add the chicken, return to the boil, pop on the saucepan lid and simmer for 10 minutes.

3  Put a kettle of water on to boil and place the dry noodles in a saucepan.

4  Add the green beans and carrot to the soup and simmer, uncovered, for a further 5 minutes.

5  At the same time, pour the boiling water over the noodles and bring to the boil. Cook for 5 minutes (or according to the manufacturer's instructions).

6  Add the coriander and spring onions to the soup. Check seasoning, and if it requires a little more salt, add a bit more fish sauce.

7  Drain the noodles and divide between 2 large, deep soup bowls.

8  Carefully pour the soup over the noodles, sprinkle the chopped chilli on top and serve with the lime wedges.

**Makes:** 4 mugs
**Prep time:** 10 minutes
**Cooking time:** 15 minutes

# butter chicken

*You need to think ahead for this recipe to give the chicken enough time in the marinade to absorb all the flavours.*

750g/26oz chicken breast, diced into
    2cm/¾ inch cubes

FOR THE MARINADE
100g/4 oz natural yoghurt
2½-cm/1 inch piece fresh ginger, peeled
    and grated (ideally with a microplane
    grater)
3 cloves garlic, crushed
4 tbsp garam masala
juice of 1 lemon

FOR THE SAUCE
100g/4oz cashew nuts
1 × 400g/14oz tin chopped tomatoes
2 medium onions, finely chopped
25g/1oz butter
6 cloves garlic, crushed
5cm/2 inch piece fresh ginger, peeled
    and grated
1 tsp garam masala
2 tbsp fennel seeds
100ml/4fl oz water
1 tsp sugar
75g/3oz butter
1 lemon, quartered, to serve
170g/6oz white rice
40g/1½oz coriander leaves, chopped

1  Make the marinade by combining all the ingredients in a medium bowl. Add the chicken cubes and stir thoroughly, making sure they are completely covered by the marinade. Cover with clingfilm and leave in the fridge for 24 hours.

2  To make the sauce, start by blitzing the cashews in a food processor until they look like powder.

3  Add the tinned tomatoes and whiz until smooth. Put to one side.

4  In a medium saucepan, gently fry the onions in the first quantity of butter. When the onions are soft, add the garlic, ginger and garam masala. Stir well and allow to fry very gently for a further couple of minutes.

5  Meanwhile, using a pestle and mortar or spice grinder, pound the fennel seeds until powered. Add to the onion mixture and cook briefly until the paste is very fragrant.

6  Pour the tomato mixture over the onions. Add the water and sugar and slowly bring to the boil.

7   Turn the heat right down and allow to simmer for 30 minutes. Keep a careful eye on the sauce and stir regularly to prevent it from sticking to the saucepan and burning. If cooking the sauce in advance, allow to cool at this point and refrigerate until ready to use.

8   When you are nearly ready to eat, preheat the grill to hot and arrange the chicken pieces on a grill pan. Grill the chicken for about 12 minutes, turning once. The chicken should be cooked and slightly charred at the edges.

9   Warm the sauce through and add the second quantity of butter. Stir gently to encourage the butter to melt.

10  When the chicken is cooked, add to the sauce. Stir well and serve with rice (cooked as directed on the packet) and lemon wedges. Sprinkle with the chopped coriander.

**Serves:** 4 adults
**Prep time:** 20 minutes
**Cooking time:** 45 minutes
**Marinating time:** 24 hours

TIP

■ The sauce can also be made in advance, which means you only need grill the chicken and cook some rice when you're ready to eat.

# sausages with lentils

This is a great way to introduce children to lentils because it combines them with that all-time children's favourite, sausages! Having said that, with the addition of the crème fraîche and mustard sauce, adults find these hard to resist too.

1 tbsp olive oil
1 medium onion, finely chopped
200g/7oz pancetta, diced
2 cloves garlic, crushed
1 large carrot, diced
1 stick celery, diced
1 tsp thyme, chopped
2 bay leaves
½ fennel bulb, finely chopped
225g/8oz Puy lentils

450ml/16fl oz water
½ chicken stock cube
1 tsp redcurrant jelly
8 large, garlicky sausages
2 tbsp crème fraîche
1 tbsp wholegrain mustard
1 tbsp balsamic vinegar
salt and pepper
40g/1½oz parsley, chopped

1  Preheat the oven to 190°C/375°F/GM5.

2  Heat the olive oil in a medium saucepan and gently fry the onion until soft. Add the cubed pancetta and garlic and continue to fry until the bacon starts to colour and the fat begins to run.

3  Add the carrot, celery, thyme, bay leaves and fennel and fry for a further 5 minutes.

4  Stir in the lentils and add the water, ½ stock cube and redcurrant jelly and stir well.

5  Bring to the boil and reduce the heat to a minimum. Put a lid on the saucepan and very gently simmer for 25–30 minutes until the lentils are cooked. The lentils must be neither mushy nor in any way grainy.

6  Meanwhile, pop the sausages into the oven and cook for about 25 minutes, turning regularly.

7  Mix together the crème fraîche and mustard and put to one side.

8  When the lentils are ready, add the balsamic vinegar and check the seasoning. Add the chopped parsley before dividing the lentils between 4 warm, shallow soup plates. Place the sausages on top and serve with the crème fraîche and mustard.

**Serves:** 4
**Prep time:** 20 minutes
**Cooking time:** 60 minutes

# minced lamb curry

A delicate introduction to curry – although I now get complaints that it's too mild! I also get requests for poppadums, but I haven't mastered them yet... This is one of those dishes that tastes even better when reheated.

2 tbsp groundnut oil
2 small onions, finely chopped
1 clove garlic, crushed
pinch of salt
900g/2lb lamb mince
3 tbsp curry powder (adjust to taste – this is how mine enjoy it and it does have quite a kick)

3 tbsp tomato purée
3 tbsp mango chutney
2 tbsp malt vinegar (I use Sarsons)
100ml/4fl oz good quality chicken stock (I use bouillon concentrated stock)
25g/1oz flaked almonds
6 dried apricots, quartered
50g/2oz sultanas
salt and pepper

1 Heat the oil in a large pan over a moderate heat. Add the onions, garlic and salt and allow the onions to soften. Add the lamb mince, breaking it up with a wooden spoon, and allow it all to colour. I usually tip out the excess fat from the lamb but for this curry I find it's best to leave it in.

2 Add the curry powder, tomato purée, chutney and vinegar and allow to cook together, stirring well. Make up the stock and add to the pan, followed by the almonds, apricots, sultanas and seasoning.

3 Allow the sauce to simmer gently for approximately 30 minutes.

4 Serve with white rice, cooked as directed on the packet.

**Serves:** 4 children, leaving enough for supper for 2
**Prep time:** 20 minutes
**Cooking time:** 30 minutes

# Laid-back Suppers

When I have a bit more time on my hands, I like to be a bit more creative in the kitchen. Most of the recipes in this section take a bit longer to prepare, but once they're on the go you can usually leave them to finish cooking in the oven whilst you wander off and do something else. It's suppers like these that I really enjoy cooking at weekends, when the pressure is off and it's just me, Gordon and the kids hanging out together at home.

Chicken and chickpeas

Tuna steaks with roasted little gem lettuces, new potatoes and tomatoes

Toad-in-the-hole with roasted shallots

Lamb cutlets and minted new potato salad

Black bean chilli with chunky guacamole and soured cream

Baked sea bass

Roasted butternut squash spaghetti lasagne

Orange chicken bake

Russian fish pie

Stuffed marrow

# chicken and chickpeas

This recipe seems to have evolved from a combination of Italian and Moroccan dishes that I've tasted. It's a very simple, one-pot dish which tastes wonderful with a loaf of crusty fresh bread and a crisp green salad.

4 tbsp olive oil
8 chicken legs
2 medium onions, chopped
200ml/7fl oz red wine
400g/14oz tin tomatoes
300ml/11fl oz chicken stock (or 300ml/
   11fl oz water and a chicken stock cube)

1 tbsp balsamic vinegar
400g/14oz tin chickpeas
large bunch basil
salt and pepper
1 head garlic, broken into individual
   cloves with the skin left on

1 Preheat the oven to 180°C/350°F/GM4.

2 On the hob, heat the oil in a casserole dish until it shimmers. Add the drumsticks and brown on all sides then remove and put to one side.

3 Turn the heat down and add the chopped onions. Stir well to make sure the onions absorb all the chicken sediment at the bottom of the pan.

4 When the onions are soft and have just started to colour, add the red wine and turn up the heat. The wine will bubble and spit, so be careful. Keep boiling until virtually all the wine has evaporated and the onions are stained red.

5 Add the tinned tomatoes, stock, balsamic vinegar and chickpeas. Rip up half the basil leaves and throw into the casserole. Season with salt and plenty of pepper, stir well and bring to the boil. Turn the heat down to a simmer and carefully arrange the drumsticks on top of the tomatoes and chickpeas.

6 Sprinkle the whole garlic cloves over the top. Cover the casserole dish with the lid and place in the oven for 30 minutes. Remove the lid and return to the oven for a further 30 minutes.

7 Sprinkle the remaining torn basil over the chicken pieces, check the seasoning and serve immediately.

**Serves:** 4
**Prep time:** 10 minutes
**Cooking time:** 1 hour

# tuna steaks with roasted little gem lettuces, new potatoes and tomatoes

100g/4oz baby new potatoes
180g/6½oz cherry vine tomatoes
extra virgin olive oil
Maldon sea salt
1 garlic clove

2 tuna steaks
salt and black pepper
2 baby little gem lettuces
juice of ½ a lemon
balsamic vinegar

1 Preheat the oven to 220°C/425°F/GM7 for the tomatoes.

2 Place the new potatoes in a pan of cold water, bring to the boil and simmer until just cooked. (You should be able to pierce them easily with the tip of a knife.) Drain and set aside.

3 As soon as you have the potatoes on to boil, get going with the tomatoes. Place them, still on the vine, onto a baking tray, drizzle over a generous amount of extra virgin olive oil, sprinkle over Maldon sea salt and grate over the garlic. Gently prick a couple of tiny holes in each tomato. Place them in the preheated oven for 15 minutes, then reduce the temperature to 150°C/300°F/GM2 and leave for a further 15 minutes.

4 When the tomatoes are on the lower heat and the potatoes are cooked, heat some olive oil in a non-stick pan until really hot and smoking slightly. Season both sides of the tuna steaks, drizzle lightly with oil and pan-fry each side for approximately 1–2 minutes.

5 Meanwhile, take your little gem lettuces, cut off the ends and remove the nice crispy leaves. Drizzle them with olive oil and season with salt and pepper. Heat some olive oil in a frying pan, then place the leaves in gently, squeezing over some lemon juice. Let the leaves wilt very slightly – you don't want them to colour and you still want them crispy so this is really just flash-frying them! Remove from the pan and lay on your serving plate.

6 Place the tuna steaks in the centre, arrange the tomatoes and potatoes to one side next to the little gem.

7 Lightly drizzle some olive oil and balsamic vinegar over the dish and serve.

Serves: 2
Prep time: 10 minutes
Cooking time: 20 minutes

# toad-in-the-hole with roasted shallots

12 chipolata sausages
6 rashers unsmoked streaky bacon, halved
400g/14oz shallots
2 tbsp balsamic vinegar
4 tbsp olive oil
salt and pepper
4 tbsp sunflower oil

FOR THE BATTER
2 eggs
125g/4½oz plain flour
300ml/11fl oz milk
1 tsp salt

1 Start by making the batter. Put the eggs, plain flour, milk and salt in a liquidizer and blend until smooth. Put to one side. Ideally, this should rest for 30 minutes, so if you're feeling very efficient you can make it in advance and leave in the fridge until needed.

2 Preheat the oven to 200°C/400°F/GM6.

3 Now set about skinning the sausages. I think it's easiest to use a pair of scissors to cut neatly along one side of the sausage skin and then just peel it off. Having cut the bacon rashers in half, wind each short piece around a sausage to give it a new skin.

4 Cut off the stalks and roots of the shallots, removing any loose skin. Don't peel them, though, because the aim is to almost steam them in their skins. Put into a large bowl and pour over the balsamic vinegar and olive oil and season with salt and pepper. Toss the shallots around until they are evenly coated. Pour out onto a baking tray and roast for 20–25 minutes.

5 Remove from the oven, allow to cool a little, then peel the outer layers off the shallots and cut into quarters.

6 Put 4 large ramekins onto a baking tray and place in the oven to heat up. After about 5 minutes, remove from the oven and put 1 tbsp of sunflower oil in each ramekin. Return to the oven for another 5 minutes until the oil is shimmering and just starting to smoke.

7 Remove the ramekins once again from the oven and put 3 sausages and a handful of shallots into the bottom of each, then divide the batter between the 4 dishes. Return to the oven and cook for 30 minutes, then serve immediately.

Serves: 4
Prep time: 20 minutes
Cooking time: 1 hour

TIP

■ This goes fantastically well with steamed tender-stem broccoli.

# lamb cutlets and minted potato salad

8 lamb chops

FOR THE MARINADE
4 cloves garlic, sliced
2 tbsp chopped rosemary
6 tbsp olive oil

FOR THE POTATO SALAD
750g/26oz new potatoes
salt
large bunch mint, chopped, plus 2 sprigs
2 garlic cloves, peeled
3 tbsp red wine vinegar
6 tbsp olive oil, plus extra for drizzling
black pepper

1 Put the chops in a large bowl and tip in the marinating ingredients. Make sure the meat is well coated with the herbs and garlic. Cover and refrigerate for at least 30 minutes.

2 Put the potatoes in a medium saucepan and cover with water. Season with a good pinch of salt and add a couple of sprigs of mint and the garlic cloves. Bring to the boil, cover and simmer for 20 minutes until tender. Drain the potatoes and remove the garlic and mint.

3 Return the saucepan to the heat briefly to allow all the remaining water to evaporate. Turn off the heat and leave the pan uncovered until the potatoes are cool enough to handle, but still warm.

4 Cut the potatoes into even sized pieces (no more than 2cm/¾ inches across) and return to the saucepan.

5 Pour over the red wine vinegar and olive oil, add the chopped mint and stir well. Season with salt and a good grinding of black pepper. Put the lid on the saucepan and leave until ready to serve.

6 Preheat the oven to 180°C/350°F/GM4.

7 Heat a frying pan over a medium-to-high heat with a splash of olive oil and fry the chops in batches for 2 minutes on each side. When they are sealed, place on a baking tray until all the chops are ready. Transfer to the oven and cook for 5 minutes.

8 Just before serving the potatoes, check the seasoning and drizzle over a little olive oil.

9 Arrange the lamb chops and potato salad on warm plates and serve with a green salad.

**Serves:** 4
**Prep time:** 15 minutes
**Marinating time:** 30 minutes to 2 hours
**Cooking time:** 30 minutes

# black bean chilli with chunky guacamole and soured cream

*I can honestly say I don't notice the absence of meat in this vegetarian dish. It's incredibly filling and easy to cook, and can be made well in advance if necessary.*

FOR THE CHILLI
4 tbsp olive oil
3 medium onions, chopped
2 celery stalks, sliced
4 garlic cloves, crushed
1 tsp chilli powder
½ tsp ground cumin
½ tsp ground coriander
1 tbsp plain flour
2 × 400g/14oz tins chopped tomatoes
1 tbsp red wine vinegar
1 tbsp tomato purée
1 bay leaf
25g/1oz bunch fresh coriander, roughly
   chopped, leaves and stalks separated

2 × 400g/14oz tins black-eyed beans
1 × 400g/14oz tin kidney or pinto beans
salt and pepper

FOR THE GUACAMOLE
½ red onion, finely chopped
4 plum tomatoes, chopped
1 lime, juiced, plus 2 limes, quartered,
   to serve
2 large, just ripe avocados
15g/½ oz bunch fresh coriander, finely
   chopped
salt and pepper

150ml/5fl oz soured cream

1  Warm the olive oil in a large enamel casserole dish and add the chopped onions. Fry for about 7 minutes until softening but not coloured. Add the celery and garlic and continue to cook for another couple of minutes.

2  Add the chilli powder, ground cumin and ground coriander and continue to fry for a further 2 minutes. Add the plain flour and stir very well, making sure the onions are all evenly coated. Stir for a minute or so before adding the tins of chopped tomatoes.

3  Add the red wine vinegar, tomato purée and bay leaf. Finely chop and add the coriander stalks. Bring to the boil, stirring all the time, before reducing the heat to a minimum. Put the lid on the casserole and leave to simmer for 20 minutes. Check it a couple of times to make sure nothing is sticking and burning at the bottom of the pan.

4  When the time is up, add all the beans, stir and bring back to the boil. Again, reduce the heat to a minimum, put the lid back on and simmer for 20 minutes to allow the beans to absorb the chilli flavours.

**5** If you are making this in advance, you can now remove the casserole from the heat and put to one side until you need it – either in the fridge or on the side, depending upon how far in advance you have made it.

**6** To make the guacamole, combine the finely chopped onion and tomatoes in a bowl with the lime juice. When you are about 30 minutes away from eating, chop up the avocados and add. Finally, add the coriander and check the seasoning.

**7** Just before serving the chilli, stir in the roughly chopped coriander leaves.

**8** Serve in warm bowls with the guacamole and soured cream spooned on top. Give extra lime wedges for people to use as they wish.

**Serves:** 4–6
**Prep time:** 30 minutes
**Cooking time:** 40 minutes

**TIP**

■ You can serve with plain boiled rice, but I don't think it's essential.

# baked sea bass

*This takes only a few minutes to prepare but tastes delicious.*

2 sea bass (weighing about 500g/18oz in total), gutted
salt and pepper
2 tsp fennel seeds
1 lemon (½ juiced, ½ thinly sliced) plus 1 lemon
   cut into wedges to serve
1 bunch fresh tarragon
1 large bulb fennel, finely sliced
2 tbsp dry vermouth (I use Noilly Prat)

**1** Preheat the oven to 180°C/350°F/GM4.

**2** Start by cutting 2 pieces of aluminium foil measuring about twice the length of the fish. Cut similar sized pieces of greaseproof paper and put 1 piece of paper on top of each piece of foil.

**3** Put 1 fish in the centre of a piece of greaseproof paper. Open the cavity and season with salt, pepper and 1 tsp fennel seeds. Repeat with the second fish.

**4** Divide the slices of lemon and the tarragon between the cavities of each fish. Scatter the slices of fennel on top of the fishes and pour 1 tbsp of vermouth over each one. Season again with salt and pepper.

**5** Take the long sides of greaseproof paper and foil and pinch together, twisting to make sure no steam will be able to escape. Finally, tightly roll up the ends of the foil until nearly touching the head and tail of the fish.

**6** Place on a baking tray and bake for 30 minutes.

**7** Remove from the oven and unwrap the fish, being careful of the scalding steam that will escape as you do so. Discard the chopped fennel, tarragon and lemon slices before transferring to warm serving plates. Garnish with lemon wedges and serve.

**Serves:** 2 adults or 4 children
**Prep time:** 15 minutes
**Cooking time:** 30 minutes

# roasted butternut squash spaghetti lasagne

*A favourite fall-back for when the kids have vegetarian friends over – my friends the Flurys approve so it must be good!*

400g/14oz butternut squash
50g/2oz butter (to roast butternut)
Maldon sea salt
black pepper
1 garlic clove, finely sliced
few sprigs of rosemary
2 tbsp olive oil (to roast butternut)
500g/18oz spinach
170g/6oz spaghetti
drizzle of olive oil to coat pasta when cooked

2 × 400g/14oz tins chopped tomatoes
2 tbsp Worcester sauce
2 tbsp soy sauce
2 tbsp fresh basil (or dried)
2 tbsp vegetable oil
1 leek, finely sliced
160ml/5½fl oz vegetable stock
50g/2oz pine nuts
150g/5oz ricotta cheese
180ml/6½fl oz single cream
75g/3oz mature Cheddar cheese, grated

1 Preheat the oven to 190ºC/375ºF/GM5.

2 Peel and dice the butternut squash and place on a roasting tray dotted with the butter. Season with salt and pepper, toss over the garlic and rosemary then drizzle over the olive oil. Roast in the oven for about 20 minutes until tender.

3 Meanwhile, steam the spinach until wilted, then lay it on kitchen roll and blot to absorb the excess water.

4 When the butternut is soft to the tip of a knife, take out and mash, discarding the garlic and rosemary. Spoon over any juices and perhaps add a little more butter if needed.

5 Cook the spaghetti as directed. Drain and run under cold water, season and drizzle with a little olive oil to stop it sticking together. Set aside.

6 For the tomato sauce, empty the tinned tomatoes into a pan, heat gently and season with black pepper. Add Worcester sauce, soy sauce and basil. Heat to a low simmer and leave simmering over a low heat.

7 Heat the vegetable oil in a medium pan and fry the leek until soft, adding a little seasoning while frying. Add the mashed butternut squash and the stock, stir occasionally and bring up to a simmer, allowing all the liquid to be absorbed.

8 Gently toast the pine nuts in a small pan until golden.

9 In a mixing bowl, mix the spinach, ricotta and cream together.

10 Spread the squash mixture over the bottom of an ovenproof dish (approx. 30cm x 20cm/12 x 8 inches and 6–7cm/2–3 inches deep).

11 Sprinkle over the pine nuts and top with half of the pasta. Spread the tomato sauce over this then lay the remaining pasta on top. Spread the spinach and ricotta on the top then sprinkle over the Cheddar cheese.

12 Place in the oven for 30 minutes until the dish is bubbling nicely.

13 You may want to lightly grill the top to add a little more colour – your choice!

**Serves:** 6
**Prep time:** 20 minutes
**Cooking time:** 50 minutes

TIP

■ If you don't fancy eating vegetarian, add either pancetta or mince to the tomato sauce.

# orange chicken bake

*Normally I don't like fruit and meat combinations, but I really love this.*

6 white potatoes
3 leeks
salt and pepper
2 oranges, peeled and thinly sliced
1.3kg/3lb chicken pieces
   (I favour skinless and boneless thighs)
dash of olive oil
3–4 sprigs of rosemary or thyme
90ml/3fl oz orange juice
100ml/4fl oz chicken stock

1 Preheat the oven to 180°C/350°F/GM4.

2 Peel the potatoes and cut into 2½ cm/1 inch chunks. Remove the ends of the leeks and roughly chop.

3 Place the potatoes and leeks mixed together in the bottom of an ovenproof dish (approx. 30cm x 20cm/12 x 8 inches and at least 7–8cm/3 inches deep), sprinkling over a little seasoning. Place the orange slices on top of the leeks and potatoes then add on the chicken pieces. Drizzle over some olive oil and season again. Place the rosemary or thyme sprigs on the top then pour over the orange juice and chicken stock.

4 Bake in the oven for approximately 1¼ hours. Check the chicken is cooked through before serving.

**Serves:** 6–8
**Prep time:** 20 minutes
**Cooking time:** 1¼ hours

TIP

■ Delicious served with crusty bread or rice.

# russian fish pie

This is a take on a Russian fish pie called koulibiac. I cannot claim that this recipe is at all authentic because I have deliberately simplified it and, true to form, used ready-made pastry rather than making my own. It is utterly delicious and can be made up to 24 hours in advance as long as you wrap it up well in clingfilm to stop it drying out.

100g/4oz basmati rice
1 tbsp sunflower oil
200ml/7fl oz water
25g/1oz butter
3 leeks, cut into 1cm/½ inch slices
1 garlic clove, crushed

250g/9oz chestnut mushrooms, sliced
700g skinned salmon fillet
15g/½oz bunch dill, chopped
200g/7oz half-fat crème fraîche
375g/13oz pack puff pastry
1 egg, beaten

1  Preheat the oven to 220°C/425°F/GM7.

2  In a small saucepan, gently fry the basmati rice in the sunflower oil. When the rice becomes translucent, add the water. Bring to the boil and allow to simmer very gently for 10 minutes, then place a tight-fitting lid on the saucepan and turn off the heat. Leave to stand for 15 minutes.

3  Melt the butter in a large sauté pan (with lid). Add the leeks and garlic and cook until soft but not coloured.

4  Add the mushrooms and stir well. When the mushrooms release their liquid, place the salmon fillet on top of the mushrooms and leeks, put on the lid, lower the heat and steam for 10 minutes.

5  Carefully remove the salmon from the sauté pan and put to one side.

6  Stir the rice into the leeks and mushrooms. Add the chopped dill and crème fraîche.

7   Taking half the pastry, roll out until you have a rectangle the same size as the piece of salmon. Place on a well-greased baking tray or, ideally, on a piece of greaseproof paper on a baking tray. Prick all over with a fork and place in the hot oven for 10 minutes or until golden brown. Remove and place on a wire rack until cool.

8   Put the cooked pastry base on a large piece of greaseproof paper and spoon half the leek and rice mixture on top, spreading it out evenly. Carefully place the salmon on top. Now spoon the remaining leek and rice mixture on top of the salmon and gently press down.

9   Roll out the remaining pastry to make a large enough piece to cover the salmon and tuck in underneath the cooked pastry base.

10  Place the pastry over the salmon and carefully lift the edges of the raw pastry. Paint the edge of the raw pastry with a little beaten egg before tucking beneath the base.

11  With a very sharp knife, cut some diagonal lines in the top of the pastry, about 4cm/ 1½ inches long.

12  Brush the entire raw pastry case with beaten egg.

13  If you want to finish cooking the pie a little later, wrap tightly with clingfilm and put to one side until needed. Otherwise, carefully lift the fish pie onto a baking tray, gripping the sides of the greaseproof paper.

14  Cook at 220°C/425°F/GM7 for 10 minutes before reducing the heat to 180°C/350°F/GM4 and cooking for a further 15 minutes.

**Serves:** 4–5
**Prep time:** 30 minutes
**Cooking time:** 25 minutes

# stuffed marrow

*You will need an ovenproof dish big enough to fit in your marrow rings – size depends on how many you are doing.*

1 large onion, finely chopped
2 garlic cloves, finely chopped
10 button mushrooms, thinly sliced
1 red pepper, seeds removed and finely
   chopped
2 sticks of celery, finely chopped
900g/2lb beef mince
sprinkling of Maldon sea salt

grinding of black pepper
2 tsp soy sauce
400g/14oz tin of tomatoes
100ml/4fl oz stock
150ml/5fl oz red wine
1 marrow
sprinkling of mature Cheddar
   cheese

1  Preheat the oven to 180°C/350°F/GM4.

2  Fry together the onions and garlic until soft, then add the mushrooms, pepper and celery and allow to soften together.

3  In a separate pan, brown the mince over a high heat and break it all up. Add this to the vegetables in the main pan. Add some salt and pepper and the soy sauce, tip in the tomatoes, stock, bay leaves and red wine and let this bubble for 5 minutes, then turn down the heat and leave to simmer for as long as possible.

4  Meanwhile, slice the very end off the marrow and cut into rings 2½ cm/1 inch thick. Remove the inner soft area and leave the centre clean for the sauce. Place these into a lightly greased ovenproof dish. Spoon in the sauce – be generous! Place in the oven for approximately 15–20 minutes.

5  Just before they are ready (the marrow should be pierced with a sharp knife to check) sprinkle over the Cheddar and allow to brown. You may prefer to grill this last bit.

6  Serve!

**Makes:** approximately 6 rings, with sauce left over for your freezer!
**Prep/cooking time:** 40 minutes to make the sauce – the longer it simmers, though, the better – then 20 minutes in the oven

# Vegetable Temptations

When it comes to vegetables, my kids still need a bit of encouragement – Jack always leaves his until last, hoping he might get away with not eating them! I find the trick is not to give up if they say they don't like one vegetable or another and to look for another way to win them round. My latest triumph has been with courgettes – though Holly still insists on calling them slimy cucumbers! I try to make my children see that it's not me against them but us working together to help them like something new. I think this is why, when they do finally like something, they feel quite proud of themselves.

The recipes in this section have all had the thumbs up from my lot and are really easy to add on as a side dish to any of the lunches or suppers in the other sections. Mix and match at will!

Carrot and parsnip mash

Roasted cauliflower and broccoli with fennel seeds

Green beans with almonds

Red cabbage with balsamic vinegar

Puy lentils

Garden peas with pancetta and roasted garlic

Spinach with cream

Sweet red onions

Carrots with star anise and orange zest

Pan-fried courgettes with garlic and parmesan

Steamed sugar snap peas with soy sauce

Roasted butternut squash with red peppers and black olives

# carrot and parsnip mash

*This can easily be made in advance and reheated in a microwave or warming drawer when needed.*

500g/18oz carrots, peeled and roughly chopped
300g/10½oz parsnips, peeled and roughly chopped
salt and pepper
75g/3oz butter
freshly grated nutmeg

1  Put the carrots, parsnips and a generous pinch of salt in a medium saucepan with a lid, cover with water and bring to the boil. Simmer for about 12 minutes, until the carrots are soft.

2  Drain and return the pan to the heat. Give the pan a shake so that any residual water evaporates.

3  Using a potato masher, pound the carrots and parsnips until almost, but not totally, smooth.

4  Add the butter and stir until melted. Check the seasoning and give a generous grinding of pepper.

5  Finally, grate some nutmeg over the mash and stir in. Don't add too much initially – taste and add more according to your preference.

**Serves:** 6 as a side dish
**Prep time:** 10 minutes
**Cooking time:** 12 minutes

TIP

■  This tastes brilliant with roast chicken or turkey.

# roasted cauliflower and broccoli with fennel seeds

*Most children I know like broccoli but not as many like cauliflower. By combining them like this, it's amazing how many will – almost by accident – discover that they like both!*

1 medium cauliflower
1 broccoli head of a similar size
1 tbsp fennel seeds
3 cloves garlic, crushed
salt and pepper
4 tbsp olive oil

1 Preheat the oven to 180°C/350°F/GM4.

2 Cut the cauliflower and broccoli into even sized florets, measuring about 2½ cm/1 inch.

3 Pound the fennel seeds with a pestle in a mortar, add the crushed garlic, a pinch of salt and the olive oil and mix together.

4 Put the cauliflower and broccoli into a large bowl and pour over the olive oil mixture.

5 Using your hands, make sure the vegetables are evenly coated with the oil, garlic and fennel before transferring to a large baking tray.

6 Scrape out the bowl, ensuring none of the precious flavours are still sitting at the bottom, and add to the vegetables.

7 Give a very good grinding of pepper before placing in the oven for 25 minutes.

8 Once during the cooking time, take the baking tray out of the oven and give it all a good shake to make sure everything is being cooked evenly.

**Serves:** 4–6 as a side dish
**Prep time:** 5 minutes
**Cooking time:** 25 minutes

# green beans with almonds

*There is a lot of lemon in this recipe which makes it a fantastic accompaniment to grilled fish.*

300g/10½oz green beans, topped and tailed
50g/2oz butter
75g/3oz flaked almonds
1 lemon, juiced

1  Place the beans in a steamer and cook for 5 minutes.

2  Meanwhile, melt the butter in a medium saucepan and add the flaked almonds. Stir constantly until the almonds are a pale brown. Don't take your eyes off the saucepan because the almonds will turn from beautifully golden to burnt cinders in a split second.

3  As soon as the almonds have reached the desired colour, pour over the lemon juice. It will spit and sizzle, so be careful.

4  Remove from the heat, stir in the cooked beans and serve immediately.

**Serves:** 4–6 as a side dish
**Prep time:** 5 minutes
**Cooking time:** 5 minutes

# red cabbage with balsamic vinegar

*This is sweet and zingy enough to be popular even with people who claim they don't like vegetables.*

75g/3oz butter
1 red cabbage, finely sliced
100ml/4fl oz balsamic vinegar
1 tbsp redcurrant jelly
salt and pepper

**1** Melt the butter in a large saucepan.

**2** Add the cabbage and toss it in the butter, making sure it is evenly coated.

**3** Add the vinegar and redcurrant jelly, and season with a little salt and pepper.

**4** Put on the lid and turn the heat down to the lowest setting.

**5** Cook for 25–30 minutes, stirring a couple of times along the way.

**Serves:** 6 as a side dish
**Prep time:** 5 minutes
**Cooking time:** 25–30 minutes

TIP

■ This tastes amazing with roast pork.

# puy lentils

Adults think that children don't like lentils but it's surprising how many love them. These can be made slightly in advance and served warm, and make a wonderful accompaniment to roast chicken and bread sauce.

1 medium onion, finely chopped
1 clove garlic, crushed
225g/8oz Puy lentils, rinsed through a sieve
450ml/16fl oz water
½ chicken stock cube
1 bay leaf
salt and pepper

1  In a medium saucepan with a close-fitting lid, put the onion, garlic, lentils, water, stock cube and bay leaf, and season with salt and pepper.

2  Bring to the boil, uncovered. Reduce to a simmer, making sure all the lentils and the bay leaf are under the water line before putting on the lid.

3  Turn the heat down to its lowest setting, using a heat diffuser if necessary, and cook, covered, for 30 minutes. The lentils should be tender but not mushy, and all but about a tbsp of liquid should have evaporated.

4  Remove from heat and keep covered until needed.

**Serves:** 4 as a side dish
**Prep time:** 5 minutes
**Cooking time:** 35 minutes

TIP

■  If there are any left over, add 1 tbsp balsamic vinegar and 1 tbsp olive oil and eat cold with grilled white fish.

# garden peas with pancetta and roasted garlic

100g/4oz garden peas (frozen or fresh)
75g/3oz cubed pancetta
knob of butter
1 small shallot, finely chopped
fresh mint, finely chopped

1 Place the peas into a pan of boiling water and cook as directed. Drain.

2 In a frying pan (there's no need to add any oil), cook the pancetta until nicely crisp. Tip out onto kitchen roll and wipe around the pan to get rid of excess grease.

3 Add the butter to the pan, fry the shallot until softened and add the pancetta and peas. Sprinkle in the fresh mint and serve.

**Serves:** 4 as a side dish
**Prep time:** 5 minutes
**Cooking time:** 10 minutes

# spinach with cream

*A lot of children don't like spinach as they find it too bitter. The cream in this recipe sweetens the spinach and goes down a treat with my lot.*

50g/2oz butter
100ml/4fl oz double cream
500g/18oz fresh spinach, thoroughly washed
   and shaken to remove most water
freshly grated nutmeg
salt and pepper

1 Melt the butter in a very large saucepan. Add the cream and warm through.

2 Cram the spinach into the saucepan and stir as best you can.

3 Place the lid on the saucepan and cook on a very low heat for 2 minutes. Remove the lid and stir well. Give a good grating of nutmeg and season with salt and pepper.

4 Turn the heat up and stir until you are left with a small amount of thick liquid.

5 Place in a food processor and pulse a couple of times but not long enough to make it into a purée. Serve immediately.

**Serves:** 4–6 as a side dish
**Prep time:** 5 minutes
**Cooking time:** 3 minutes

# sweet red onions

6–8 medium red onions
25g/1oz unsalted butter
1 tbsp olive oil
couple of rosemary sprigs
salt flakes and pepper
5 tbsp balsamic vinegar

1  Preheat the oven to 140°C/275°F/GM1.

2  Peel the onions and slice off a third of the tops to expose the layers.

3  Heat the butter and olive oil in a heavy-based ovenproof pan. Add the onions, cut side down, and sauté for 4–5 minutes until golden brown. Add the rosemary and seasoning. Deglaze the pan with the balsamic vinegar, cover with foil and transfer to the oven.

4  Slowly roast the onions for 30 minutes, then remove the foil and turn the onions over.

5  Return the pan to the oven for 1–1¼ hours until the onions are tender. Check halfway through as you may need to add a few tbsp of water if the balsamic vinegar begins to catch and burn.

6  To test if it's ready, pierce the middle of the thickest onion with a small knife. If cooked, it should meet with little resistance. Spoon over the syrupy glaze and serve the onions warm.

**Serves:** 6 people
**Preparation time:** 15 minutes
**Cooking time:** 1½ hours

# carrots with star anise and orange zest

*Carrots are usually quite popular with children but the orange twist in this adds a little extra pizzazz for a Sunday lunch.*

8 large carrots
15g/½oz butter
2 tbsp olive oil
2 star anise
2 tsp runny honey
zest of 1 orange

1  Peel the carrots and slice diagonally into ½ cm/¼ inch pieces. Place in a pan of boiling water for 5 minutes, then drain.

2  Heat the butter and olive oil in a pan, add the star anise and the carrots, then drizzle over the honey and sprinkle on the orange zest. Stir it all together to heat through gently. Remove the star anise and serve immediately.

**Serves:** 4 (as a side dish)
**Prep time:** 5 minutes
**Cooking time:** 8–10 minutes

# pan-fried courgettes with garlic and parmesan

*My kids don't like courgettes – they call them slimy cucumbers! This is the only way I can get them to eat courgettes without hiding them in sauces.*

2½ tbsp olive oil
3 courgettes, cut into ½ cm/¼ inch slices
2 garlic cloves, finely chopped
zest of 1 lemon
juice of ½ lemon
50g/2oz freshly grated Parmesan
black pepper
Maldon sea salt

1 Heat the oil in a frying pan then add the courgettes. Sprinkle over the garlic and lemon zest and squeeze in the lemon juice.

2 Without crushing the courgette slices, turn them over and shake the pan to keep them moving and stop them catching on the bottom.

3 After a couple of minutes, sprinkle over half of the Parmesan, shaking the pan again to spread it throughout the courgettes. Add a grinding of black pepper and a sprinkle of salt. The courgettes should cook for no longer than 5 minutes. They should still have a good bite to them and a slightly golden colour.

4 Sprinkle in the last of the Parmesan, let it begin to melt and serve.

**Serves:** 4–6 as a side dish
**Prep time:** 10 minutes
**Cooking time:** 5–7 minutes

# steamed sugar snap peas with soy sauce

My children love edamame beans but these can be hard to come by unless you have a Chinese supermarket on your street corner, so I have substituted them with sugar snap peas which are naturally sweet and tasty.

150g/5oz sugar snap peas
2 tbsp soy sauce
sprinkle of Maldon sea salt (optional)

1 Top and tail the sugar snap peas, pulling off the tough string from the side.

2 Place in the top of a steamer for 1½ minutes.

3 Serve with a small bowl of soy sauce and salt flakes as a dip, or to sprinkle over.

**Serves:** 4 as a side dish
**Prep time:** 5 minutes
**Cooking time:** 1½ minutes

# roasted butternut squash with red peppers and black olives

1 butternut squash, peeled, deseeded and diced
olive oil, to drizzle over
2 garlic cloves, finely sliced
couple of rosemary sprigs
2 red peppers, stalks and seeds removed, quartered
10 marinated black pitted olives
salt and pepper

**1** Preheat the oven to 190°C/375°F/GM5.

**2** Arrange the butternut squash on a lightly greased oven tray. Drizzle over olive oil, sprinkle over the garlic slices, add the rosemary sprigs and season. Place in the oven.

**3** After approximately 15 minutes, add the red peppers and the olives, drizzle over a little more oil, season and return to the oven for a further 15 minutes.

**4** Serve immediately.

**Serves:** 4–6 as a side dish
**Prep time:** 15 minutes
**Cooking time:** 30 minutes

# Big Family Lunches

Having lots of people around for lunch can be really intimidating, especially if you're trying to impress the in-laws! My strategy is to cook something that I can pretty much prepare in advance (preferably the night before) and then, closer to the time, shove in the oven and leave to cook. This is particularly handy if you have to tidy up the house, make sure the kids are all ready on time, and find the time to get glammed up yourself! These recipes are some of my favourites.

Marinated topside with Jerusalem artichoke and potato mash

Mini trout fillets with cucumber dressing

Pumpkin soup

Summer gammon with roasted pineapple and red onion and coriander salsa

Slow-cooked Moroccan leg of lamb with lemon couscous

Baked sea trout

Beef Wellington

Roast pork with fennel stuffing and simple apple sauce

# marinated topside with jerusalem artichoke and potato mash

Marinating this relatively inexpensive cut of beef for 24 hours prior to roasting it tenderizes the meat and imparts such an intense flavour that you almost forget you're not eating fillet! I usually serve this with a watercress salad to cut through the richness of the potato and winey gravy.

750g/26oz piece topside, trimmed

FOR THE MARINADE
3 medium onions, quartered
1 tbsp juniper berries, slightly crushed
2 carrots, cut into chunks
2 celery stalks, sliced
4 garlic cloves, thickly sliced
1 tsp peppercorns
3 bay leaves
1 small bunch thyme
1 bottle red wine

FOR THE GRAVY
2 tsp blackcurrant jelly
½ quality beef stock cube
15g/½oz soft butter
1 tsp cornflour
salt and pepper

FOR THE MASH
400g/14oz potatoes, peeled and cut into even sized chunks
400g/14oz Jerusalem artichokes, peeled
pinch of salt
300ml/11fl oz milk
50g/2oz butter

1 The day before you are planning to eat this meal, find a medium bowl and place the piece of topside in it surrounded by all the chopped vegetables and herbs for the marinade. Pour over the bottle of wine, cover with clingfilm and pop in the fridge. If the wine doesn't completely cover the meat, remember to turn the meat over from time to time, just to make sure it all has a chance to soak up the flavours.

2 If possible, remove the meat from the fridge an hour before cooking to allow it to come to room temperature.

3 Preheat the oven to 170ºC/325ºF/GM3.

4 Take the meat out of the marinade and pat dry. Pour the marinade – vegetables, herbs and all – into a large saucepan and slowly bring to the boil. Simmer for 30 minutes.

5  Place a frying pan on a hot hob and brown the meat on all sides. Place on a roasting tray and cook for 1 hour.

6  When the meat has been in the oven for about 20 minutes, put the potatoes and Jerusalem artichokes in a saucepan of water with a pinch of salt, and bring to the boil. Reduce the heat and simmer for 20 minutes until soft. Drain and return to the saucepan over a low heat to allow any excess water to evaporate. Using a potato ricer (ideally) or a masher, mash the potatoes and artichokes until very smooth. Push them to one half of the saucepan and pour the milk and butter into the other half. Put the half of the saucepan containing the milk over a low heat and bring to simmering point. Stir everything together and taste for seasoning, adding more salt if necessary. Keep warm until needed.

7  Now it's time to return to the bubbling pot of marinade. Once it has simmered for about 30 minutes, pass through a sieve and discard all the vegetables and herbs. Return the liquid to the saucepan and continue to simmer gently. Stir in the blackcurrant jelly and ½ stock cube and allow to dissolve. In a cup, mix together the soft butter and cornflour until you have a smooth paste. I now leave the gravy until the meat is ready.

8  When the beef has cooked for about 35 minutes, remove from the oven and place on a warm plate to rest for 10 minutes.

9  Meanwhile, bring the gravy back to boiling point and stir in the butter and cornflour paste. Keep stirring until it has all dissolved and the gravy has thickened. Check the seasoning and add salt and pepper if necessary.

10  Thinly slice the beef and serve on warm plates with the mashed potato and gravy.


**Serves:** 4
**Prep time:** 20 minutes
**Marinating time:** 24 hours
**Cooking time:** 1 hour


TIP

■  If Jerusalem artichokes aren't in season, use 800g/28oz potatoes instead.

# mini trout fillets with cucumber dressing

*I'm very lucky to have a lovely fishmonger who fillets and skins my trout for me and I'd recommend that it's a job best done by a professional!*

4 rainbow trout, filleted and skinned
100ml/4fl oz white wine vinegar
200ml/7fl oz water
2 lemons, juiced
2 large shallots, finely chopped
5cm/2 inch piece root ginger, finely
  chopped
5 garlic cloves, thinly sliced
2 tsp sugar

FOR THE CUCUMBER DRESSING
½ cucumber, peeled, deseeded, finely chopped
3 limes, juiced
50ml/1¾fl oz water
2 tbsp fish sauce
2 garlic cloves, finely chopped
2 tsp caster sugar
25g/1oz bunch coriander, finely chopped
pepper

1   Make sure that the trout fillets are free of any tiny bones. You can buy special fish tweezers to remove the bones, or use normal ones – just make sure you disinfect them.

2   Combine the white wine vinegar, water, lemon juice, chopped shallots, ginger, garlic and sugar in a small saucepan, bring to the boil then take off the heat and set aside to cool.

3   Roll each fillet up from the tail end and place in a round ovenproof dish (18cm/7 inch diameter) on its side, like Swiss roll. The trout fillets should pack quite tightly into the dish to stop them unravelling. When the liquid has cooled, pour over the fish and leave to marinate for about 2 hours. If you are preparing in advance, you can leave the fish for up to 24 hours in the fridge.

4   When you are ready to cook, preheat the oven to 180°C/350°F/GM4. Cover the dish with foil and place in the oven for 40 minutes. Then remove from the oven and allow to cool.

5   For the dressing, combine the ingredients in a jam jar with a tight-fitting lid and shake well.

6   To serve, remove the fillets from the cooking liquid and spoon the cucumber sauce over the top. Serve with a crispy salad.

**Serves:** 4 as a starter, 1 fillet per person
**Prep time:** 15 minutes
**Marinating time:** 2 hours
**Cooking time:** 40 minutes

# pumpkin soup

*This rich, heart-warming soup always goes down a treat.*

1 tbsp olive oil
15g/½oz butter
2kg/4½lb pumpkin, peeled and diced
3 sprigs of rosemary, stems kept on
3 garlic cloves, peeled and finely chopped
1–2 Parmesan crusts
1 litre/1¾ pints chicken stock
sprinkle of Maldon sea salt
fresh Parmesan, to garnish (optional)

1  Heat the oil and butter in a large pan, then add the diced pumpkin, rosemary and garlic along with the Parmesan crusts. Let the crusts melt a little and the pumpkin start to colour slightly before adding your stock and salt. Let everything simmer together gently for approximately half an hour.

2  Carefully remove all the rosemary and the Parmesan crusts and pour or spoon the soup into your liquidizer. Liquidize until smooth then return to the pan and warm over a low heat to ensure it is hot enough.

3  Serve, if desired, with a couple of fresh Parmesan shavings on the top.

**Makes:** 6 large mugs
**Prep time:** 20 minutes
**Cooking time:** 1 hour

TIP

- This is a great way of using up any old Parmesan crusts you may have saved. You can freeze them until you need them.

# summer gammon with roasted pineapple and red onion and coriander salsa

Although we tend to associate gammon with Christmas, cooked like this it really is a wonderful sunshine meal. Serve with new potatoes and a crisp salad for an easy and delicious summer feast. Some people say it's unnecessary to pre-boil the gammon joint but, if nothing else, it's a great way of getting rid of a load of scum, so I prefer the old-fashioned way!

2kg/4½lb unsmoked gammon joint
2 litres/3½ pints pineapple juice
1 large onion, peeled and halved

FOR THE SALSA
1 small red onion, peeled and finely chopped
1 red chilli, deseeded and finely chopped
1 fresh pineapple, weighing about 1kg/2¼lb, peeled and cut into chunks
2 limes, juiced
25g/1oz coriander, chopped
salt and pepper

1 Put the gammon in a large saucepan and cover with cold water. Bring to the boil before carefully removing the heavy joint and discarding the water.

2 Wash out the saucepan well, return the joint to the pan and pour over the pineapple juice. Add the halved onion. If the top of the gammon is sticking up above the liquid by more than a couple of centimetres, add some water to bring the level up.

3 Reduce the heat to a very gentle simmer. Put on the lid and cook for 2 hours. Periodically, check to make sure the liquid level is still high, topping up with boiling water if necessary.

4 When the meat has about ½ hour to go, make the salsa. Mix together the finely chopped onion and chilli. Stir in the pineapple chunks and lime juice. Finally, add the coriander and seasoning.

**5** When the gammon's time is up, carefully remove from the cooking liquid. Carve off the fat layer and discard before slicing the meat into thin pieces. Arrange on plates with a spoonful of salsa on the side.

**Serves:** 8
**Prep time:** 10 minutes
**Cooking time:** 2 hours 20 minutes

**TIP**

- Cartons of pineapple juice are readily available in supermarkets, and in dire emergencies you could always substitute the fresh pineapple in the salsa with the tinned variety!

# slow-cooked moroccan leg of lamb with lemon couscous

I use the term 'Moroccan' in its very loosest sense! The harissa paste and couscous give it a certain North African feel but I'm not trying to pass this off as an authentic Moroccan dish. Make it in the morning of the day you need it and just let it sit on the side until it's time to reheat it gently. You'll need a very large enamel casserole with a tight-fitting lid. It must be large enough to accommodate the leg of lamb – you may need to ask your butcher to trim the bone down.

600g/21oz onions, peeled and quartered
8 garlic cloves, peeled
3 celery sticks, roughly chopped
1 large leek, roughly chopped
2½kg/5½lb leg of lamb
3 tbsp olive oil, plus more as necessary
3 aubergines, halved lengthways and cut into 2cm/¾ inch slices
½ tsp ground cinnamon
2 level tbsp harissa paste
3 tbsp tomato purée

3 × 400g/14oz tins chopped tomatoes
500ml/18fl oz water
large bunch coriander, roughly chopped
250ml/9fl oz natural full-fat yoghurt

FOR THE COUSCOUS
250g/9oz dried couscous
pinch of salt
boiling water to cover
25g/1oz butter
zest of 2 lemons

1 Preheat the oven to 170ºC/325ºF/GM3.

2 Put the onions, garlic, celery and leek into a food processor and pulse until very finely chopped. You can, of course, do this by hand but the food processor saves masses of time.

3 Dry the lamb with kitchen roll.

4 Over a medium to high heat, heat the olive oil in the casserole on the hob. Brown the lamb on all sides, being careful of spitting hot fat. Remove from the casserole and put to one side.

5  Reduce the heat a little and fry the aubergine slices in batches until brown on all sides then transfer to a plate. During this process you may need to add more olive oil as the aubergines really soak it up.

6  Add a little more olive oil and spoon in the finely chopped onion mixture. Stir well to remove all the sediment from the bottom of the pan.

7  Add the ground cinnamon and cook, stirring all the time, for about 5 minutes.

8  Stir in the harissa paste and tomato purée and cook for a further 2 minutes.

9  Return the lamb to the casserole, followed by the aubergine.

10  Pour over the tinned tomatoes and enough water to more or less cover the meat.

11  Bring to the boil, place the lid on the casserole and transfer to the oven. Cook for 2 hours.

12  About ½ hour before the lamb is due to come out of the oven, prepare the couscous. Put the couscous in a heatproof bowl and add a pinch of salt. Pour over boiling water until it is just covered. Add the butter, cover the bowl with clingfilm and leave for 10 minutes. Remove the clingfilm and stir the couscous with a fork until fluffy. Grate on the lemon zest and stir again. Check seasoning and add a little more salt if necessary.

13  When the lamb is ready, remove from the casserole and carve with a sharp knife. The meat should be very tender. Put a large spoonful of couscous on a plate beside the slices of lamb, spoon over the aubergine sauce and sprinkle with coriander. Serve with a bowl of yoghurt for people to dollop on as they wish.

**Serves:** 6
**Prep time:** 20 minutes
**Cooking time:** 2 hours 10 minutes

TIPS

- Harissa paste, a fiery North African chilli-paste, is increasingly available on supermarket spice shelves and can be bought easily online.

- This also works well with half a leg of mutton used in place of the lamb.

# baked sea trout

Sea trout comes into season in April which makes it perfect food for a springtime lunch, anticipating all the fun of summer to come. It has a wonderful flavour and texture and is large enough to feed six or eight people easily. What makes it even more special is that it is fantastic value for money and very simple to prepare. Although sea trout are not available from supermarkets, your local fishmonger, I am sure, will always be delighted to order one in for you. Serve with mayonnaise mixed with crushed garlic and lemon juice.

2kg/4½lb sea trout, gutted, fins removed
olive oil
salt and pepper
2 lemons, thinly sliced

15g/½oz bunch of dill
large bunch of flat-leaf parsley
50ml/1¾fl oz white wine
lemon wedges and watercress,
  to garnish

1 Preheat the oven to 200°C/400°F/GM6.

2 Tear off a sheet of wide, tough foil, about 15cm/6 inches longer than the fish itself. Drizzle a little olive oil over it and spread around well.

3 Place the fish in the centre of the foil and season well inside with salt and pepper. Proceed to stuff the cavity with half of the sliced lemon, the dill and most of the parsley. Pour the white wine into the cavity, as much as that is possible!

4 Arrange the remaining lemon slices and herbs over the trout. Season the top of the fish with salt and pepper and pour over a good glug of olive oil.

5 Draw up the foil around the fish and fold and pinch the ends together tightly. Leave as much space inside the foil as possible to allow the steam to circulate around the fish while it cooks.

6 Place in the oven for 45 minutes. Check the fish is cooked by looking at its eyes – if they are no longer glassy but milky white, the fish is done. If you don't think it's quite cooked, seal the foil again and return to the oven for another 5 minutes.

7  When the fish is cooked, allow it to cool before carefully lifting from the foil. Discard all the lemon slices and cooking herbs. Serve at room temperature on a large plate garnished with lemon wedges and watercress.

**Serves:** 6–8
**Prep time:** 10 minutes
**Cooking time:** 45–50 minutes (plus time to cool)

TIP

- This is also a delicious way of cooking ordinary rainbow trout. Simply reduce the cooking time to about 20 minutes, depending on the size of the fish.

# beef wellington

This is an undeniably expensive dish but you sometimes you need to push the boat out for a big family celebration! Its huge advantage is that you can prepare it the night before, giving it the final 30-minute blast in the oven as and when you are ready to eat. Wrapping the beef in the pancakes first keeps the pastry crisp and golden. (You can buy ready-made pancakes if you don't want to make your own.) If you prefer, you can make your own chicken liver pâté, but having tried it both ways, I just don't think it's worth the extra work and washing up.

FOR THE WELLINGTON
1½kg/3½lb piece of beef fillet
freshly ground black pepper and
    salt flakes
6 tbsp olive oil
40g/1½oz butter
200g/7oz button mushrooms, thinly
    sliced
150g/5oz pack quality chicken liver pâté
1 × 500g packet of puff pastry
plain flour for rolling pastry
1 egg, beaten

FOR THE PANCAKES
125g/4½oz plain flour
1 egg
pinch of salt
300ml/11fl oz milk
1 tbsp chopped parsley
1 tbsp vegetable oil

1  Preheat the oven to 190°C/375°F/GM5.

2  Season the beef well with salt and pepper. Heat 15g/½oz of the butter and 3 tbsp of the oil in a heavy baking tray until it shimmers. Carefully – because it will spit – place the meat in the tray, drizzle over the remaining 3 tbsp of oil, and brown it on all sides.

3  Place the tray with the beef in the preheated oven and roast for 20 minutes (for rare, which I think is best). Remove from the oven and allow to cool.

4  Melt the remaining butter in a small saucepan and cook the mushrooms until soft and all the excess moisture has cooked off. Tip into a mixing bowl and set aside to cool.

5  Now for the pancakes. Sieve the flour into a bowl. Create a well in the centre, then add the egg and salt. Start to whisk together, gradually adding the milk until you have a smooth batter. Stir in the chopped parsley.

**6** Place a sheet of greaseproof paper onto a large plate, and cut off another similar-sized square of paper. You will need to stack the pancakes between sheets of greaseproof paper.

**7** Heat the vegetable oil in a small frying pan until the oil shimmers. Add a small ladle of the batter to cover the base and cook for 1–2 minutes until golden underneath. Flip over and cook for a further 1–2 minutes.

**8** Turn out onto the plate and cover with the second sheet of greaseproof paper.

**9** Spoon another ladle of batter into the pan and repeat until you have used up all the batter, adding a little more oil to the pan as necessary. You actually only need four pancakes for this recipe, but you can freeze the others for future use. Set aside to cool.

**10** Return to your mushrooms and mix them together with the chicken liver pâté to form a thick paste.

**11** Roll out the pastry until it is large enough to wrap around the beef. Lay two pancakes on the raw pastry and spread over the pâté and mushroom mixture.

**12** Place the beef in the middle of the pancakes then cover with two more pancakes. Brush the edges of the pastry with beaten egg, then wrap the pastry around the beef, placing the seal underneath. Trim off the four corners of raw pastry. If you are feeling creative, cut the pastry ends into leaf shapes to decorate the top of the Wellington – brush with beaten egg to 'glue' them to the beef.

**13** Brush the entire pastry case with beaten egg and – if you are finishing it off later – wrap very closely with clingfilm so that it doesn't dry out while waiting to be cooked.

**14** When ready to cook, reheat the oven to 190ºC/375ºF/GM5 (if necessary). Remove the clingfilm and place the fillet on a greased baking tray.

**15** Cook for 30 minutes until the pastry is a rich gold and shining. Serve immediately.

**Serves:** 8–10
**Prep time:** 45 minutes
**Cooking time:** 1 hour

TIPS

- Serve straight from the oven, carved into 1cm/½ inch slices.

- Eat with seasonal vegetables and perhaps a creamy potato dauphinoise.

# roast pork with fennel stuffing and simple apple sauce

*This tastes equally good hot – with roast potatoes and all the trimmings – or cold with salad. It isn't hard to get really crisp crackling but you do have to think ahead a little so that the meat has time to get to room temperature and the skin dries thoroughly in the open. Serve with apple sauce, of course!*

1¾kg/4lb pork loin with skin scored
1 tbsp olive oil
salt and pepper

FOR THE STUFFING
1 large shallot, peeled
1 fennel bulb
1 small Bramley apple, cored and peeled
4 garlic cloves, peeled
1 tbsp fennel seeds
salt and pepper

FOR THE APPLE SAUCE
2 Bramley apples
water
40g/1½oz butter
salt and pepper

1  Begin by preparing the stuffing. It really couldn't be easier, particularly if you have a food processor to hand! Put the shallot, fennel, apple and garlic into the food processor and pulse until very finely chopped. Stir in the fennel seeds and season well with salt and pepper.

2  If the pork loin is already tied up, you will need to untie it in order to stuff the meat. Lay it flat and, at the thickest part of the meat, cut a slit with a very sharp knife to create a pocket to hold the stuffing. Make the pocket as large as you can without cutting it open.

3  Push as much of the stuffing as possible into the pocket and then fold the thinner end of the meat over to seal in the stuffing.

4  This is the slightly fiddly, messy bit! Using butcher's string, carefully tie the meat together as tightly as possible to seal the stuffing in the centre of the joint. You will probably need to tie about 6 tight loops around the meat in all.

**5** Place the pork on a wire rack above a baking tray, skin-side uppermost. Using kitchen paper, blot the skin dry. Now leave on the kitchen surface for at least 30 minutes.

**6** Preheat the oven to 220°C/425°F/GM7.

**7** Just before placing in the oven, rub the olive oil into the pork skin and season with salt and pepper.

**8** Put the pork in the oven and set the kitchen timer for 30 minutes. When the half hour is up, turn the oven down to 190°C/375°F/GM5 and cook for a further hour and 10 minutes, until the juices run clear when you pierce it with a skewer.

**9** While the pork is cooking, make the apple sauce. Peel, core and slice the apples and put in a small saucepan, adding enough water just to cover them. Bring to the boil then turn down the heat so that it is barely simmering. Cover with a lid and let it simmer for about 10 minutes until the apples are so soft that they break up when stirred. Stir in the butter and mix well, seasoning with salt and pepper. Taste to check the seasoning and add a little more butter if you think it necessary.

**10** When the pork is ready, remove from the oven and leave to rest for 15 minutes before carving.

**Serves:** 6
**Prep time:** 20 minutes
**Cooking time:** 1 hour 40 minutes

# Baking Adventures

Nothing beats the smell of baking – it brings back so many happy memories from my childhood. I used to help Mum make fairy cakes and I think this must be why I still like making them best of all.

Baking must be the easiest way to get children excited about food and cooking, whether it's a sneaky finger in the cake mixture, kneading dough or getting messy icing biscuits – the perfect antidote for wet afternoons. I can't say that I always have the time to bake – it seems to be more of a treat than a necessity – but there is such a lot of enthusiasm when there's freshly baked bread or a slice of cake for tea that I wish I did it a little more often!

Tomato and basil focaccia

Spelt bread

Coconut 'naan' bread

Marmite focaccia

Chelsea buns

Apricot and walnut bread

Bakewell slice

Double chocolate brownies

Orange polenta cake

Fruit cake

Rock cakes

Jam tarts

Anzac biscuits

Lamington cakes

# tomato and basil focaccia

**FOR THE DOUGH**
250ml/9fl oz water
3 tbsp olive oil
1½ tsp Maldon sea salt
400g/14oz white bread flour
2¼ tsp dried yeast
6 ice cubes

**FOR THE TOPPING**
10 cherry tomatoes, halved
large handful of basil leaves, torn
25g/1oz grated Parmesan
olive oil for drizzling
Maldon sea salt and freshly ground
    black pepper, to taste

1 Place all the ingredients for the dough into a bowl and mix together (use a mixer with a dough hook if possible). When it is in a nice dough ball, knead on a lightly floured surface for approximately 5 minutes. Use the heel of one hand to push the dough away from you, simultaneously using the other hand to bring the dough back to the starting position.

2 Place the dough in a greased mixing bowl and leave to rise in a warm place for approximately 45 minutes, until it has doubled in size.

3 Preheat the oven to 190°C/375°F/GM5.

4 Lightly grease a 33 x 23cm (13 x 9 inch) baking tin.

5 Knead the dough on a floured surface, adding half the tomatoes and half of the torn basil leaves. Knead to mix through evenly.

6 Place the dough into the baking tin, stretch it over the bottom and even it out. Using your fingers, dimple the top of the dough. Top with the remaining basil and tomatoes, pushing them a little into the dough. Sprinkle over the Parmesan cheese. Drizzle over the olive oil, letting it make 'pools' in the finger dents. Sprinkle over some Maldon sea salt and ground black pepper.

7 Place in the bottom third of the oven. Put 6 ice cubes in the bottom of the oven to create some steam, and leave to bake for 25 minutes until golden brown. Remove and slice into 12 pieces.

**Makes:** 12 pieces
**Prep time:** 60 minutes (45 minutes for resting the dough)
**Cooking time:** 25 minutes

# spelt bread

Spelt is an ancient grain that has enjoyed something of a comeback in recent years. It contains more protein, fat and fibre than wheat and has a delicious, nutty flavour. Another huge advantage is that, despite its high gluten content, it can be tolerated by some people who are intolerant to gluten in normal wheat bread.

500g/18oz spelt flour
7g/¼oz sachet easy yeast
1 tsp salt
300ml/11fl oz warm water
1 tbsp olive oil
2 tbsp honey
2 tbsp rosemary, chopped, plus some for sprinkling
Maldon sea salt for sprinkling

1  Tip the flour, yeast and salt into a large bowl and make a well in the middle. Slowly pour the warm water into the well and stir with a wooden spoon until the mixture is almost completely combined.

2  Add the olive oil, honey and chopped rosemary and mix well.

3  Turn the dough out onto a floured work surface and begin kneading by using the heel of one hand to push the dough away from you, simultaneously using the other hand to bring the dough back to the starting position. Continue to knead the dough for 10 minutes.

4  Place the dough in a large, greased bowl, cover with a clean tea towel and leave in a warm place for an hour to rise.

5  Once the dough has doubled in size, remove it from the bowl and knead again. This time you don't have to knead it for very long; you simply want to knock out the air in the dough, which will take seconds rather than minutes.

6  Preheat the oven to 220°C/425°F/GM7.

7 Form the dough into a circle-shaped loaf and place on a greased baking tray. Cut a cross in the top of the loaf and sprinkle with a little flaked salt and some rosemary.

8 Return to a warm place and leave to rise again for 15 minutes.

9 Put the loaf in the preheated oven and bake for 35–40 minutes. To tell if the bread is ready, carefully pick it up and tap the bottom of the loaf. If it sounds hollow you know it is ready.

10 Put the bread on a cooling rack as soon as it comes out of the oven to ensure that the crust is crisp.

**Makes:** 1 loaf
**Prep time:** 1 hour 45 minutes
**Cooking time:** 35–40 minutes

# coconut 'naan' bread

This is in no way an authentic naan bread recipe but it is easy to make. It's also quick because it doesn't use yeast and therefore doesn't need time to rise. These are easy and fun for children to make, and a great way of encouraging them to embrace new flavours.

450g/1lb plain flour
2 tsp baking powder
1 tsp salt
125ml/4½fl oz milk, plus 2 tbsp extra
   for brushing

125ml/4½fl oz natural yoghurt
1 egg
25g/1oz desiccated coconut
25g/1oz ground almonds
1 tsp caster sugar
5 tbsp water

1 Preheat the oven to 220°C/425°F/GM7.

2 Sieve the flour and baking powder together in a large mixing bowl. Add the salt.

3 In another bowl, beat together the milk, yoghurt and egg.

4 In a third bowl, mix together the coconut, almonds, sugar and water to make a paste. Put to one side.

5 Make a well in the middle of the flour and pour the milk mixture into it. Using a wooden spoon, carefully mix together the flour and liquid until they are a dough.

6 Turn the dough out onto a lightly floured surface and knead for 3–4 minutes until the dough has a silky smooth texture. Use the heel of one hand to push the dough away from you, simultaneously using the other hand to bring the dough back to the starting position.

7 Divide the dough into 4 or 6 balls, depending on how many individual pieces of bread you want.

8 Take one of the small dough balls and flatten in between your hands. In the centre of the slightly crooked circle you have created, place a dessertspoon-sized pile of the coconut mixture. Fold the dough in half to cover the coconut and pinch down the sides to seal it in. With either a rolling pin or your hands, shape the dough into a tear-drop shape.

9 Brush with a little milk before placing on a lightly greased, preheated baking tray and cooking for 5–7 minutes until golden.

10 Serve as soon as possible.

**Serves:** 4
**Prep time:** 10–15 minutes
**Cooking time:** 5–7 minutes

TIP

- Once you've removed the cooked naan from the oven, place on a clean napkin or tea towel and lightly fold the corners in to keep the bread warm.

# marmite focaccia

*A delicious and simple recipe ... unless you hate Marmite, in which case try the tomato and basil focaccia instead!*

FOR THE DOUGH
250ml/9fl oz water
3 tbsp olive oil
1½ tsp Maldon salt
400g/14oz white bread flour
2¼ tsp dry yeast

FOR THE TOPPING
olive oil for drizzling
4 tsp Marmite
2 tsp water

6 ice cubes

1 Mix all the dough ingredients together in a bowl, using a mixer and a dough hook if you have one, then knead on a lightly floured surface for approximately 5 minutes. Use the heel of one hand to push the dough away from you, simultaneously using the other hand to bring the dough back to the starting position.

2 Place the dough in a lightly greased mixing bowl and leave to rise in a warm place for approximately 45 minutes, until it has doubled in size.

3 Preheat the oven to 190°C/375°F/GM5.

4 Lightly grease a 33 x 23cm (13 x 9 inch) baking tin.

5 Place the dough into the baking tin, stretch over the bottom and even it out. Using your fingers, dimple the top of the dough. Drizzle over the olive oil, letting it make some 'pools' in the finger dents.

6 Place the Marmite and water in a bowl over a pan of boiling water and allow the Marmite to soften until it is easy to stir.

7 Using a pastry brush, paint the melted Marmite generously over the surface of the focaccia dough.

8 Place in the bottom third of the oven. Put 6 ice cubes in the bottom of the oven to create some steam and leave to bake for 25 minutes until golden brown.

Makes: 12 pieces
Prep time: 60 minutes (45 minutes for resting the dough)
Cooking time: 25 minutes

# chelsea buns

These remind me so much of my childhood. This recipe might seem quite daunting but it is deceptively easy and quick (if you don't count the time it takes the dough to rise), and the results are incredibly satisfying!

**FOR THE YEAST MIXTURE**
2 × 7g/½oz sachets dried yeast
1 tbsp plain flour
1 tsp caster sugar
375ml/13fl oz warm milk

**FOR THE DOUGH**
550g/1¼lb plain flour
1 tbsp caster sugar
½ tsp ground cinnamon
¼ tsp ground nutmeg
½ tsp mixed spice
50g/2oz butter
1 egg

**FOR THE FILLING**
50g/2oz butter
25g/1oz soft brown sugar
100g/4oz currants
100g/4oz sultanas

**FOR THE ICING**
50g/2oz caster sugar
1 tbsp water

1  Begin by waking up the yeast! Put the yeast, flour and sugar in a small bowl and slowly pour in the warm milk, stirring all the time. Put to one side for 10 minutes until frothy.

2  Put the dry ingredients for the dough into the bowl of an electric mixer.

3  Melt the butter.

4  When the yeast mixture is ready, pour into the mixer bowl containing the flour, sugar and spices. Add the melted butter and egg. Turn the mixer on at its lowest setting and leave to work for 10 minutes. Alternatively, if you fancy some stress-busting kneading and some good exercise for bingo wings, turn the mixture out onto a well-floured surface and use your hands to knead for 10 minutes instead!

5  Place the dough in a large, greased bowl, cover with a clean tea towel and leave in a warm place for 1 hour until it has doubled in size.

6   While this is happening, make the filling simply by melting the butter in a medium-sized saucepan, stirring in the brown sugar and finally the dried fruit. Put to one side until needed.

7   When the dough has risen sufficiently, turn it out onto a floured surface and knead for a minute.

8   Roll the dough out into a flat rectangle measuring approximately 20 x 40cm/8 x 16 inches.

9   Spread the fruit filling evenly over the dough, leaving a 2cm/¾ inch border. Carefully roll it up, starting from the longest side.

10   Cut the long roll into 9 pieces and arrange the slices, cut side uppermost, in 2 greased 23cm/9 inch round cake tins.

11   Cover and leave in a warm place for a further 30 minutes while the dough rises a little. Preheat the oven to 180°C/350°F/GM4.

12   Make the icing by mixing together the caster sugar and water. Spread over the buns and bake for 30 minutes then leave to cool in the tins for 10 minutes before transferring to a wire rack.

**Makes:** 9 buns
**Prep time:** 2 hours 15 minutes
**Cooking time:** 30 minutes

TIP

- You can make the buns by hand, but it's far quicker and easier to use the electric mixer with the dough hook attachment.

# apricot and walnut bread

This dense bread is fantastic eaten as hot buttered toast. It's a brilliant after-school teatime snack that keeps children going until supper.

250g/9oz dried apricots, roughly chopped
1 Earl Grey teabag
450ml/16fl oz water
75g/3oz oats, plus 2 tbsp extra for
   sprinkling
2 eggs, lightly beaten

150g/5oz golden caster sugar
500g/18oz self-raising flour
1 tsp salt
1 tbsp baking powder
100ml/4fl oz milk
100g/4oz walnut pieces

1 Preheat the oven to 170°C/325°F/GM3.

2 Put the dried apricots, tea bag and water into a small saucepan and bring to the boil. Simmer very gently for 5 minutes then turn off the heat and remove the tea bag. Stir in the first quantity of oats before covering with a lid. Allow to cool.

3 In the bowl of an electric mixer, beat together the eggs and sugar.

4 Sieve the flour, salt and baking powder together before adding to the egg mixture with the motor running on its lowest setting. Add the cooled apricot mixture and milk and continue to mix until completely combined.

5 Turn the motor off before adding the walnuts. Fold in with a metal spoon so as not to break the walnuts up too much.

6 Spoon into two 900g/2lb loaf tins, lined with greaseproof paper, and sprinkle with the remaining oats then bake in the oven for 1–1¼ hours. The bread will be cooked when the surface is cracked and a skewer, when inserted into the loaf, comes out clean.

**Makes:** 2 loaves
**Prep time:** 20 minutes
**Cooking time:** 1–1¼ hours

TIP

■ I always think it's best to make a couple of loaves and freeze one for another day.

# bakewell slice

*This traditional recipe is definitely a favourite with my lot. It keeps really well too – two days at best, three if you can resist!*

1 × 375g pack of shortcrust pastry
8 tbsp raspberry jam
170g/6oz unsalted butter, softened
200g/8oz caster sugar
4 large eggs, beaten
2 tbsp lemon juice
1 tsp almond extract
250g/110oz ground almonds
50g/2oz flaked almonds
Icing sugar, to dust

1  Roll out the pastry until it is approximately 3mm/1/8 inch thick. Line a 22cm/9 inch tart tin and trim the edges with a knife. Chill in the fridge for ½ hour.

2  Preheat the oven to 190°C/375°F/GM5. Prick the base of the pastry, add some baking beans or dried pasta then bake blind for approximately 15 minutes. Remove the baking beans and place the pastry back in the oven to lightly colour for 5 minutes. Remove and allow to cool.

3  Spread the jam over the pastry and start to make the filling. Beat together the butter and sugar until pale and fluffy. Slowly add the eggs and the lemon juice. Add the almond extract and fold in the ground almonds.

4  Spoon the mixture over the jam base and spread evenly. Sprinkle over the flaked almonds. Place on a baking sheet and bake for 30–35 minutes until the filling is golden on top and feels firm in the middle. If the pastry starts to get too brown, cover with foil.

5  Remove and allow to cool.

6  Dust lightly with icing sugar. When totally cool, slice into rectangles.

**Makes:** 12 slices
**Prep time:** 20 minutes
**Cooking time:** 15 minutes to bake blind the pastry plus 30–35 minutes

# double chocolate brownies

*These are quite simply the best brownies ever! Fantastic served warm from the oven with a blob of vanilla ice cream or cold as a lunchbox treat or after-school snack.*

**DARK CHOCOLATE MIXTURE**
200g/7oz good quality cooking chocolate
200g/7oz butter
250g/9oz caster sugar
3 eggs
125g/4½oz plain flour

**WHITE CHOCOLATE MIXTURE**
1 egg
200g/7oz cream cheese
50g/2oz caster sugar
1 tsp vanilla extract
100g/4oz white chocolate, broken into pieces

1 Preheat the oven to 180°C/350°F/GM4. Grease a 23cm/9 inch square brownie tin and line with greaseproof paper, making sure no brownie mixture can leak out of the tin.

2 Now make the dark chocolate mixture. Melt the dark chocolate and butter either in a microwave or a warming drawer or by placing in a heatproof bowl sitting on top of a saucepan of just-simmering water. Stir well to make sure the melted butter and chocolate are combined. Allow to cool slightly.

3 While the butter and chocolate are melting, make the white chocolate mixture. In a medium bowl, whisk together the egg, cream cheese, caster sugar and vanilla extract until completely smooth. Sir in the white chocolate pieces, then put to one side.

4 Returning to the dark chocolate mixture, whisk together the caster sugar and eggs in a third, large bowl. With the motor of the whisk still running, gently pour in the melted chocolate and butter. Carefully fold in the flour with a metal spoon.

5 Pour half the dark chocolate mixture into the brownie tin. Then pour over the much runnier white chocolate mixture. Finally, dollop in the remaining dark chocolate mixture, making sure it is evenly distributed across the whole tin.

6 With the handle of a wooden spoon, lightly stir the contents of the tin, making broad swirls. Don't over-mix or you will lose the distinction between the two colours.

7 Bake for 35 minutes. Remove from the oven and allow to cool in the tin before cutting into squares.

**Makes:** 12
**Prep time:** 20 minutes
**Cooking time:** 35 minutes

# orange polenta cake

*This lovely fruity cake is ideal for anyone with a wheat intolerance because it contains no flour.*

**FOR THE CAKE**
2 oranges
5 eggs
250g/9oz golden caster sugar
100g/4oz polenta
100g/4oz ground almonds
1 tsp baking powder

**FOR THE ICING**
1 lemon, juiced
1 orange, juiced
3 tbsp granulated
  sugar

1  Wash the oranges and place in a medium-sized saucepan. Cover completely with water and bring to the boil, then simmer for an hour. Allow to cool before removing the oranges.

2  Quarter the oranges and remove the pips. If you have a food processor, blitz the oranges until they are well-chopped but not a sludge. If you don't have a food processor, simply cut the oranges into very small pieces, making sure not to lose any of the juice. Put to one side.

3  Preheat the oven to 170°C/325°F/GM3.

4  In a large bowl, whisk together the eggs and the sugar. Fold in the polenta, ground almonds, baking powder and oranges. Carefully pour into a 25cm/10 inch spring-form tin, base and sides lined with greaseproof paper.

5  This mixture is very runny, so be careful when placing it in the oven. Cook for 1 hour then test to see if the cake is ready by inserting a skewer. If the skewer comes out clean, it is ready.

6  While the cake is cooking, make the icing by mixing together the lemon and orange juice and the granulated sugar. As soon as the cake comes out of the oven, pour the liquid over the hot cake. Allow the cake to cool in the tin.

**Serves:** 8
**Prep time:** 15 minutes
**Cooking time:** 2 hours

**TIP**

■  This cake keeps beautifully in an airtight tin for at least two days, so can easily be made in advance.

# fruit cake

When you have an unexpected visitor, there's nothing better than being able to offer them a cup of tea and a slice of homemade fruit cake. This one will keep for over a week. Wrap it tightly in tin foil and store in an airtight container.

150g/5oz butter
300g/10½oz sultanas
300g/10½oz currants
150g/5oz soft brown sugar
1 tsp ground allspice
1 tsp ground cinnamon
1 tsp ground ginger
1 lemon, zest and juice

1 orange, zest and juice (the juices of the lemon and orange should total 250ml/9fl oz; if you are a bit short, top up with water)
2 eggs, beaten
200g/7oz self-raising flour
1 tsp baking powder
100g/4oz ground almonds

1 Preheat the oven to 170°C/325°F/GM3.

2 Grease and line a 20–23cm/8–9 inch cake tin. Make a second circle of greaseproof paper to protect the top of the cake while cooking.

3 Put the butter, sultanas, currants, sugar, spices, fruit juices and zest into a medium saucepan and bring to the boil, stirring regularly. As soon as it starts to boil, pour into a large mixing bowl and allow to cool.

4 Once the mixture is completely cool, beat in the eggs.

5 Sieve together the flour and baking powder and add to the mixture, stirring thoroughly.

6 Add the ground almonds and give it final stir to make sure everything is thoroughly mixed together. Spoon into the prepared baking tin. Take the second circle of greaseproof paper and crumple it up. Smooth it out slightly and very gently rest it on the top of the cake.

7 Cook for 1 hour. To check whether the cake is cooked, insert a skewer into the centre – if it comes out clean it is ready. If not, return the cake to the oven and cook for a further 5–10 minutes before testing again.

8 Remove from the oven and place the tin on a wire rack until cool.

**Serves:** 8–10
**Prep time:** 30 minutes
**Cooking time:** 1 hour

# rock cakes

As soon as I smell rock cakes in the oven it reminds me of my childhood. My mum always used to make this exact recipe, and I would never change it!

225g/8oz plain flour
100g/4oz unsalted butter
50g/2oz currants
50g/2oz soft brown sugar
1 large egg
1 tsp baking powder
1 tsp ground cinnamon
1 tsp milk

1 Preheat the oven to 180°C/350°F/GM4.

2 Lightly grease a baking sheet.

3 Place all the ingredients in a large bowl and mix together well. Using your hands, make smallish mounds, dividing the mixture into 8. Place these mounds onto the baking sheet.

4 Bake for 10–15 minutes until the tops are a light golden brown. Don't allow them to overcook as they'll continue to cook slightly when taken out of the oven.

5 Remove from the oven and place on a cooling rack.

**Makes:** 8 (I like generous-sized cakes!)
**Prep time:** 15 minutes
**Cooking time:** 10–15 minutes

## TIPS

- Soak the currants in a shallow bowl of water to plump them up a little.

- You could replace the currants with dried cranberries.

# jam tarts

*Quite possibly the simplest treats to make – these really are a childhood classic. A nice twist of different jams makes it a little special. I tend to make larger jam tarts then cut them into four and let the children enjoy the different flavours. You can use whichever size pastry cases you prefer.*

**225g/8oz sweet pastry (I buy ready-made)**
**370g/13oz strawberry jam**

1 Preheat the oven to 180°C/350°F/GM4.

2 Roll out the pastry to a thickness of approximately ½ cm/¼ inch. Divide between four 12cm/4¾ inch lightly greased pastry cases with fluted edge and removable base, and line the tins, gently pressing down into the fluted sides. Line the pastry with greaseproof paper and add some baking beans or dried pasta. Place in the oven and bake the pastry until it is just starting to turn golden brown. This takes about 15 minutes.

3 Remove and allow to cool. Turn up the oven to 190°C/375°F/GM5.

4 Spoon in the jam, dividing it between the four pastry cases. Place them back in the oven for approximately 15–20 minutes, when the jam should be gently bubbling and the pastry golden.

5 Remove and allow to cool on a wire rack. The jam does get incredibly hot so take care not to eat until cooler.

**Makes:** 4 large jam tarts
**Prep time:** 15 minutes
**Cooking time:** 15–20 minutes

**TIPS**

- This is also delicious with lemon curd.

- Try raspberry jam – the seeds give a little more texture.

Jack'z

# anzac biscuits

I love these traditional Australian biscuits. They are thought to date back to the time of World War I when mothers made them for their boys heading off to the front line: hence the name, Australia and New Zealand Army Corps. I've tried several recipes but like this one the best.

100g/4oz plain flour
100g/4oz light brown sugar
100g/4oz desiccated coconut
150g/5oz rolled oats
100g/4oz butter
2 tbsp golden syrup
½ tsp bicarbonate of soda
2 tbsp boiling water

1  Lightly grease a baking tray large enough to hold 12 well-spaced biscuits. Preheat the oven to 180°C/350°F/GM4.

2  Mix together the flour, sugar, coconut and oats in a large mixing bowl.

3  Melt together the butter and golden syrup in a small saucepan over a low heat.

4  Dissolve the bicarbonate of soda in the boiling water then add to the butter and golden syrup.

5  Make a well in the centre of the flour mix then stir in the liquid.

6  Place teaspoon-sized mounds of the mixture on the baking tray and bake for approximately 15–20 minutes. Transfer to a cooling rack as soon as they are cooked to prevent them over-cooking underneath.

7  Best stored in an airtight container – if you can stop them disappearing from the cooling rack!

**Makes:** approximately 12 biscuits
**Prep time:** 15 minutes
**Cooking time:** 15–20 minutes

# lamington cakes

*These taste best the day you make them although they will keep for up to three days in an airtight container.*

FOR THE SPONGE
3 eggs
75g/3oz caster sugar
125g/4½oz self-raising flour
25g/1oz cornflour
3 tbsp hot water
25g/1oz butter, softened

FOR THE CHOCOLATE ICING
500g/18oz icing sugar
75g/3oz cocoa
15g/½oz butter, softened
125ml/4½fl oz milk
450g/1lb desiccated coconut

1 Preheat the oven to 180°C/350°F/GM4.

2 Lightly grease an 18 x 28cm/7 x 11 inch tin, and line with greaseproof paper.

3 Beat together the eggs until they are nice and thick and creamy. Gradually beat in the sugar until it is all dissolved.

4 Sieve in the flour and cornflour and gradually add the water and butter, stirring until you have a smooth consistency.

5 Pour the mixture into your lined and greased tin. Bake for 30 minutes then remove and place on a wire cooling rack, allowing to cool completely.

6 Now for the chocolate icing! Sieve together the icing sugar and cocoa in a bowl. Mix in the soft butter and milk, and whisk together until completely smooth. Put the bowl over a pan of hot water and stir until the icing looks silky and glossy. Add another splash of milk if the chocolate icing is too stiff.

7 Remove the greaseproof paper from the sponge square and cut it into 16 even squares of approximately 5cm/2 inches. Trim off the golden edges very carefully so you can see only white sponge.

8 Using a fork as a spear, dip each sponge square into the icing until completely covered. Sprinkle with the desiccated coconut till evenly covered. Leave the cakes and allow the icing to set … then indulge!

**Makes:** 16 squares
**Prep time:** 20 minutes
**Cooking time:** 30 minutes

# Devilish Desserts

Life without desserts would be an empty one indeed!
I love exchanging conspiratorial smiles around the
table when you all dig into to a really wicked dessert.
Some of my favourite family moments are caught
up in puddings – everybody's relaxed, the stories are
flowing and everything makes you laugh.

Cheats' summer pudding

Tom's bomb

Lemon golden syrup steam puddings

Raspberry ripple ice cream

Cinnamon and nutmeg ice cream

Children's chocolate mousse

Mango tart

Lemon and vanilla cheesecake

Lemon cake with roasted figs

Rhubarb fool

Strawberry meringue cake

Profiterole mountain

# cheats' summer pudding

*Unless you live in the middle of the countryside and grow your own soft fruits, the idea of making a summer pudding can sometimes seem too much like hard work. Despite my best efforts to the contrary, it's sometimes easier to reach for the packet of frozen fruit in the freezer. This version of the classic English pudding never fails to find an appreciative audience, and allows you to enjoy summer throughout the year!*

700g/25oz frozen summer fruit (frozen weight)
60ml/2fl oz crème de cassis
1 tbsp caster sugar
9 slices medium sliced white bread, slightly stale,
   crusts removed

1 Warm the frozen fruit in a saucepan with the crème de cassis and sugar. Keep on a low heat and be very careful not to stir too much or the fruits will break down and become red sludge rather than individual berries.

2 As they melt, the fruits will release a great deal of juice. Once you are confident the fruit has melted, drain through a sieve, being careful not to lose any of the precious juice.

3 Take a slice of bread and dunk it in the fruit juice, then place it at the bottom of a 1.2 litre/ 2 pint pudding basin. Continue to dip the stale bread in the juice and line the basin with the bread, overlapping each piece by about 1cm/½ inch. When the sides and base of the basin are completely lined, spoon in the fruit. Gently push the fruit down with the back of a metal spoon, but not hard enough to crush it.

4 Dunk the remaining bread in the fruit juice and lay it on top of the fruit to form a lid. Turn the bread which is lining the sides down to seal in the fruit. Keep any remaining juice in the fridge until you are ready to serve the pudding.

5 Place a small plate on top of the pudding basin and weigh it down, preferably with some old-fashioned kitchen weights, but if they're not readily available, a couple of tins of baked beans will do the job.

6 Place in the fridge for 24 hours (48 hours at the most) before turning out the summer pudding onto a large plate. Do this by putting the plate upside down on top of the bowl and then turning the whole thing upside down. If the pudding doesn't flop onto the plate easily, you may need to poke a palette knife gingerly around the edge before trying again.

7 Pour the remaining juice over the top of the pudding before cutting into slices and serving with double cream or vanilla ice cream.

**Serves:** 6–8
**Prep time:** 30 minutes
**Chilling time:** 24 hours

# tom's bomb

I wrote this recipe after a request from a young friend. He tasted my raspberry meringue bomb and suggested I should write a chocolate version. In an attempt to please, I came up with this, which I hope will hit the spot.

200g/7oz good quality dark chocolate
125ml/4½fl oz double cream
275ml/10fl oz whipping cream
125g/4½ oz ready-made meringues
125g/4½ oz Maltesers

1  Break the chocolate into a heat-proof bowl and pour over the double cream. Place above a saucepan of barely simmering water, making sure the bottom of the bowl doesn't touch the water.

2  While the chocolate and cream are melting, whisk the whipping cream until it just starts to thicken. A balloon whisk is preferable to an electric whisk on this occasion as it gives you much more control, making it much harder to over-whip the cream.

3  In another bowl, crumble the meringues, squeezing them in your fists to make large, chunky pieces.

4  When the chocolate has melted, stir together with the whipping cream to make a smooth, silky sauce.

5  Pour over the meringues and mix gently until they are evenly coated.

6  Finally, add the Maltesers to the meringue and cream mixture and stir in. Be careful not to stir too much because you want the pudding to be a contrasting black and white rather than a uniform brown.

7  Pour into a 1.2 litre/2 pint pudding basin, cover with foil and freeze for at least 3 hours.

8  To serve, place the pudding basin in a bowl of hot water for about 30 seconds, then tip out onto a serving plate and cut into slices.

Serves: 6 hungry children
Prep time: 20 minutes
Chilling time: 3 hours

# lemon golden syrup steam puddings

You cannot help but be reminded of school dinner desserts with this one, although they were not quite as tasty and you certainly didn't have the luxury of individual portions – more like a chunk thrown onto your plate!

170g/6oz self-raising flour
50g/2oz butter
25g/1oz caster sugar
zest of 2 lemons
90ml/3fl oz milk
90ml/3fl oz golden syrup
3 tbsp water
2 tbsp lemon juice

1 Sieve the flour into a large mixing bowl. Rub in the butter till it resembles fine breadcrumbs then stir through the sugar and lemon zest. Add the milk and mix thoroughly.

2 Lightly grease four individual 150ml/¼ pint plastic pudding basins with fitted lids with butter. Place a circle of greaseproof paper in the bottom of each basin. Spoon 1 tsp of golden syrup into each pudding basin then divide the sponge mixture between the basins. Put on the lids and place in a steamer for approximately 45 minutes.

3 Just before your puddings are ready, make the sauce. Put the rest of the syrup into a small saucepan along with the water and heat together gently, stirring through. Allow to simmer for 2–3 minutes then stir in the lemon juice.

4 Turn out the puddings onto warm plates. Pour over the sauce just before serving.

**Makes:** 4 mini puddings
**Preparation time:** 15 minutes
**Cooking time:** 45 minutes

# raspberry ripple ice cream

*Megan used to be very reluctant to try raspberries until I came up with this ice cream... the rest is history!*

600ml/1 pint double cream
300ml/11fl oz full fat milk
1 vanilla pod, sliced open and seeds removed
6 egg yolks (keep your whites for meringues
   at a later date)
50g/2oz caster sugar
300g/10½oz raspberries
icing sugar, to taste

1  Place the cream, milk and vanilla seeds into a saucepan and heat together, stirring gently, until just about to come to the boil.

2  In a bowl whisk the egg yolks and sugar until the sugar has dissolved and it has a lovely thick and creamy texture. Pour the cream and milk mixture into the bowl, whisking constantly.

3  Pour the entire mixture back into the saucepan and return to the heat. Using a wooden spoon, stir constantly until the mixture starts to thicken (check by seeing if it's coating the back of your spoon). This takes 10–15 minutes. Pour the mixture into a clean bowl and leave to cool completely.

4  Pour the mixture into a Tupperware container, put on the lid or cover with clingfilm and place in the freezer.

5  After approximately 2 hours remove the ice cream from the freezer and stir it through, bringing all the frozen edges into the middle and mixing thoroughly.

6  Return it to the freezer and repeat this procedure a couple of times at intervals of about 2 hours. When the ice cream really starts to come together, make and add the purée.

7  Take the raspberries and purée until smooth, then put through a sieve to remove the pips. Add a little icing sugar and adjust until this makes the raspberries nice and sweet and takes away the sharpness they sometimes can have. Spoon the raspberry purée into the thickened ice cream mixture and 'ripple' throughout. Return to the freezer and leave overnight.

**Serves:** 6 hungry children
**Preparation time:** 30 minutes, followed by freezing and stirring at 3 2-hour intervals
**Freezing time:** overnight

# cinnamon and nutmeg ice cream

This is a wonderful winter ice cream which works beautifully with chocolate and nuts. Although it's a very straightforward recipe, it requires a little thinking in advance. I recommend using an ice cream maker, although you don't need to buy a hugely expensive one. Mine cost under £50 and works by churning the 'custard' in a pre-frozen bowl.

250ml/9fl oz milk
1 litre/1¾ pints whipping cream
2 cinnamon sticks
½ clove nutmeg, grated (preferably with a microplane grater)
10 egg yolks
100g/4oz caster sugar

1  Put the milk and cream into a saucepan with the cinnamon sticks and grated nutmeg. Gently bring to simmering point and take off the heat. Cover and leave for several hours to let the flavours infuse.

2  In a separate bowl, beat together the egg yolks and caster sugar.

3  When the milk and cream are ready, remove the cinnamon sticks and return to the heat until nearly, but not quite, boiling.

4  Pour the hot cream over the eggs and sugar, beating with a hand-held balloon whisk all the time. Wash the saucepan before returning the egg and cream mixture to it.

5  Cook gently on a low heat, stirring all the time to prevent the mixture curdling, until it has thickened to the consistency of a thick custard. It should take about 10 minutes to achieve this, but at all times make sure it never reaches boiling point. As soon as you are happy with the thickness, pour into the freezing ice cream bowl. It is important never to stop stirring the mixture as this will make it go lumpy.

6  Set the ice cream maker to churn until frozen. Eat immediately or transfer into a suitable container and place in the freezer until needed.

**Makes:** enough for a 1½ litre/2½ pint ice cream maker
**Prep time:** 30 minutes
**Chilling time:** overnight

# children's chocolate mousse

This is a very simple chocolate mousse recipe. For adults, you could zing it up with a couple of tablespoons of rum mixed into the melted chocolate, but I don't think it needs it. Obviously, this recipe includes raw eggs, so please don't serve it to pregnant women or very young children. I also think it's important to use good quality, preferably organic, eggs.

**340g/12oz Bourneville chocolate**
**6 eggs**

1 Melt the chocolate in a heatproof bowl above a saucepan of barely simmering water, making sure the bottom of the bowl isn't touching the water.

2 Separate the eggs and divide the whites and yolks between 2 large mixing bowls. Whisk the egg whites until they form stiff peaks when you remove the whisk.

3 When the chocolate has melted, allow it to cool for a couple of minutes before stirring into the egg yolks. (If the chocolate is too hot, it will cook the yolks, making the mixture too dense to achieve the desired results.)

5 Take 2 tbsp of the beaten egg white and stir into the chocolate mixture. This will loosen the chocolate, making it much easier to move on to the next stage.

6 Add about half the remaining egg white to the chocolate, gently folding it in with a large metal spoon. With large, sweeping movements, use the spoon to cut through the egg white and bring the chocolate mixture around it. After each stroke with the spoon, twist the bowl a quarter turn, and continue until the egg whites have been completely absorbed into the chocolate. Spoon in the remaining egg white and repeat the process.

8 Carefully pour the mousse into 6 glass tumblers or coffee cups and place in the fridge for at least 2 hours.

**Serves:** 6
**Prep time:** 20 minutes
**Chilling time:** 2 hours

TIP

- This pudding can also be made a day in advance, which is another great selling point!

# mango tart

Mango is a great fruit to use with pastry as it's so full of juice, even when cooked. This comforting, soothing dessert is fantastic served when the tart is still warm — allow the mango juice to mix with a scoop of vanilla ice cream.

370g/13oz sweet pastry
1 large ripe mango
100ml/4fl oz milk
2 tbsp Demerara sugar

1 Preheat the oven to 190°C/375°F/GM5 and lightly grease a baking sheet.

2 Dust your work surface with flour and roll out the pastry until approximately ½ cm/¼ inch thick and in a circle approximately 27cm/10½ inches in diameter.

3 Transfer the pastry circle to the baking sheet.

4 Peel the mango and slice off the soft flesh thinly. Do this on a plate to retain all the mango juice.

5 Arrange the mango slices in the centre of the pastry circle. Use the soft messy flesh from around the stone for the base and the neater slices for the top. Leave a border of about 5cm/2 inches. Fold up the pastry edges over the mango to form a rough crust, leaving the centre visible.

6 Brush the pastry with milk and sprinkle the tart with Demerara sugar.

7 Bake for approximately 20 minutes until golden brown.

8 Serve warm alongside a nice big scoop of vanilla ice cream.

**Serves:** 4 children
**Prep time:** 20 minutes
**Cooking time:** 20 minutes

# lemon and vanilla cheesecake

*This is easy to make and lasts for a good couple of days without compromising on quality.*

FOR THE BASE
50g/2oz softened unsalted butter
150g/5oz digestive biscuits

FOR THE TOPPING
300ml/11fl oz sour cream

FOR THE FILLING
340g/12oz full-fat cream cheese
   (I use Philadelphia)
150g/5oz golden caster sugar
4 medium eggs
zest and juice of 1 lemon
2 tsp vanilla extract
1 vanilla pod
handful of raisins

1 Preheat the oven to 180ºC/350ºF/GM4.

2 Start making the base by melting the butter in a small saucepan.

3 Break the digestive biscuits into chunks and place in the food processor. Whiz until they are in small crumbs. If you don't have a food processor, enjoy crushing them with the back of a spoon or hammering with a rolling pin! Place into a mixing bowl and add the melted butter. Stir until all the crumbs are evenly coated.

4 Press the mixture into the bottom of a lightly greased 20cm/8 inch cake tin with removable collar, making sure you push it well into the edges.

5 Place all the ingredients for the filling, except the raisins, into the mixing bowl of the food mixer, or use a spoon to mix together by hand. Mix until smooth then stir in the raisins. Pour this mixture onto the biscuit base.

6 Bake for approximately 30 minutes until just set. It does firm up a little once removed and cooling.

7 Cool for 10 minutes then smooth the sour cream over the top. Return to the oven and cook for a further 10 minutes.

8 Remove and allow to cool and set. Remove the collar, slide off the base and place on a dessert serving plate.

9 Refrigerate the cheesecake and serve chilled.

**Makes:** 12 slices
**Preparation time:** 30 minutes
**Cooking time:** 40 minutes

TIP

- Delicious served with warmed frozen berries – see page 4.

- This recipe is adaptable in many ways. I often use cranberries instead of raisins, or even apricots chopped into little pieces.

# lemon cake with roasted figs

*There's something deeply reassuring and welcoming about sharing a pudding with a group of friends. This pudding works because of the contrast between the old-fashioned flavours of the cake and the syrupy-sweet figs. It's a wonderful summer pudding when figs are in season and children can be bribed to gather lavender flowers in the morning dew.*

FOR THE CAKE
2 lemons, juice and zest
2 tbsp lavender flowers
170g/6oz butter, at room temperature
170g/6oz caster sugar, plus 1 tbsp
3 large eggs, beaten
275g/10oz plain flour
½ tsp baking powder

FOR THE FIGS
12 fresh figs
50g/2oz Demerara sugar
2 tbsp lavender flowers
200ml/7fl oz port
crème fraîche, to serve

1 Preheat the oven to 170°C/325°F/GM3.

2 Grease and line a 20cm/8 inch springform cake tin.

3 Start by making the cake. Put the lemon juice, lemon zest and lavender flowers into a small saucepan and bring to the boil. As soon as the lemon juice starts bubbling, take off the heat, cover with a lid and put to one side to cool.

4 Cream together the butter and sugar in a large bowl using the electric hand whisk. When the mixture turns pale and drops off a spoon easily, start to add the beaten eggs, a little at a time.

5 Sieve the flour and baking powder together and add to the mixture, 4 tbsp at a time. At this stage, do not turn the motor of the electric whisk above the lowest setting.

6 Using a large metal spoon, fold the lemon juice and lavender flowers into the mixture.

7 Spoon the mixture into the prepared cake tin and bake for 40–45 minutes.

8 Check whether the cake is ready by inserting a skewer into the centre. If the skewer comes out clean, the cake is cooked. If not, return it to the oven and test again after 5 minutes.

9 Immediately after taking the cake out of the oven, sprinkle with 1 tbsp caster sugar.

10 Keep the cake in its tin for 10 minutes after removing it from the oven. After 10 minutes, turn it out onto a wire rack and allow to cool completely before storing in an airtight container until needed.

11 Increase the oven temperature to 200°C/400°F/GM6.

12 Cut the stalks off the figs and cut a cross about 2cm/¾ inch deep into the top of each fruit.

13 Lightly grease a small baking dish and arrange the figs tightly in it.

14 Mix together the Demerara sugar and lavender flowers. Sprinkle over the figs. Finally, pour over the port.

15 Roast in the oven for 20 minutes, basting the figs with the port and sugar halfway through.

16 Serve a slice of lavender and lemon cake with 1 or 2 figs, a spoonful of crème fraîche and a spoonful of the port juices poured over the top.

**Serves:** 6
**Prep time:** 30 minutes
**Cooking time:** 40–45 minutes for the cake
plus 20 minutes for the figs

**TIPS**

■ You can buy lavender flowers in some health food shops or online.

■ The figs are incredibly easy to make and can be prepared in advance then cooked when needed.

■ I always think this pudding tastes best when the figs are hot, although there is nothing stopping you from serving them at room temperature.

■ The cake can be made up to a day in advance and kept in an airtight tin once completely cooled.

# rhubarb fool

This pudding is so easy that it hardly merits being a recipe. However, it's a great way of introducing a wonderfully English, seasonal crop to a younger audience, and the fresh taste and rich colour brighten even the most miserable March mood.

800g/28oz rhubarb
25g/1oz butter
2 tbsp runny honey
2 tbsp soft brown sugar
500g/18oz Greek yoghurt

1   Heat the oven to 200°C/400°F/GM6.

2   Chop the rhubarb into 10cm/4 inch chunks and arrange in a well-buttered ovenproof dish. Drizzle over the honey and sprinkle with the brown sugar.

3   Roast in the oven for 20 minutes until the rhubarb is cooked and beginning to colour.

4   Allow to cool slightly before blitzing in a food processor until completely smooth.

5   Fold in the yoghurt and check for sweetness. You may want to add a little more honey, depending on how tart you enjoy the flavour.

6   Pour into individual glasses and refrigerate. Serve within a couple of hours.

**Serves:** 4–6
**Prep time:** 20 minutes
**Cooking time:** 20 minutes

# strawberry meringue cake

*This wicked dessert is also a wonderful alternative for a birthday cake, particularly for girls who feel they are slightly too sophisticated for traditional pink iced cakes! To save time, make the meringue discs a day or two before you need them.*

4 large egg whites
225g/8oz caster sugar
400g/14oz fresh strawberries
275ml/10fl oz double cream
1 tbsp icing sugar

1 Preheat the oven to 110°C/225°F/GM¼.

2 Find a plate measuring 20cm/8 inches in diameter and draw around it on 3 separate pieces of greaseproof paper.

3 Place the egg whites in a large bowl and whisk until they form stiff peaks. Gradually whisk in the sugar, a couple of tbsp at a time.

4 Divide the mixture equally between 3 baking sheets lined with the greaseproof paper circles, spreading the meringue out to fill the space within the marked circles.

5 Place in the oven and bake for 1 hour 40 minutes, then turn the oven off and leave the meringue discs in there until cold. Meanwhile, put a third of the strawberries in the food processor and blitz until smooth. Slice the remaining strawberries into 4 or 5 pieces each.

6 Whip the cream until it has thickened so it just holds its shape, then combine the strawberry purée, whipped cream and strawberry pieces.

7 Put 1 of the meringue discs on a serving plate and spread with half the strawberry mixture.

8 Put the next disc on top before spreading that with the remaining strawberry mixture. Place the final meringue disc on top. Place in the fridge for a maximum of 2 hours to allow the strawberry flavours to permeate the meringue. Any longer will result in the meringue going soggy. Before serving, sieve a little icing sugar onto the top. Cut into thin slices with a sharp serrated knife.

**Serves:** 6
**Prep time:** 45 minutes
**Cooking time:** 1 hour 40 minutes (plus 1–2 hours chilling time)

# profiterole mountain

*This is a little kitsch homage to my childhood memories of the 1970s which really should be shared with the next generation.*

75g/3oz butter
225ml/8fl oz water
100g/4oz plain flour, sieved
1 tsp sugar
3 medium eggs, beaten

200g/7oz good quality plain
  chocolate
125ml/4½fl oz double cream
200ml/7fl oz whipping cream
1 tbsp icing sugar

1 Preheat the oven to 200°C/400°F/GM6.

2 Put the butter and water in a medium saucepan and bring slowly to the boil. As soon as the liquid is boiling really fast, tip in all the flour and sugar and take the pan off the heat.

3 Stirring as fast as you can, beat the mixture with a wooden spoon. It will quickly become thick and glossy and come away from the sides of the pan.

4 Stand the saucepan in a basin of cold water to cool the mixture down quickly. When the mixture is cool, beat in the eggs a little at a time. The final mixture should be smooth and shiny and should drop off the spoon slowly, rather than being runny.

5 Place teaspoons of choux pastry on 2 baking sheets lined with greaseproof paper, keeping each blob about 8cm/3 inches apart. Bake for 20–30 minutes until crisp and golden brown. Remove from the oven. Taking a skewer, make a pea-sized hole in the bottom of each profiterole and leave them upside down. Return to the oven and cook for a further 5 minutes. This will stop them being soggy on the inside. Place on a wire rack and cool.

6 Place the chocolate and double cream in a heatproof bowl above a saucepan of barely simmering water. When the chocolate has melted, stir well to make a rich sauce.

7 Whip together the whipping cream and icing sugar until thick.

8 Just before serving, slice each choux bun in half and fill with the whipped cream. Stack on a serving plate to make a great mountain and pour over the chocolate sauce.

**Serves:** 6–8
**Prep time:** 30 minutes
**Cooking time:** 25–35 minutes

# acknowledgements

Megan, Jack, Holly and Matilda, thank you, guys, for being my favourite critics and for taking part. Thanks too for (almost always) waiting before devouring. I love you all.

Gordon, thank you for your patience and for letting me use your kitchen – thank God I cracked the combination lock!

Mum, thanks for your never-ending support and ideas – you're always ready with a solution when I've messed up.

Olly, Diane and Helen, a million thanks for your testing and tasting.

Alex, thank you for always being ready with fantastic coffee and marmite on toast. You've been such a fantastic support and working with you again has been such fun.

Wei, Deirdre and Jenny, thank you once again for a great job.

Jacqui, you've done it again with your amazing design. I know I've pushed your patience to the limit with my delays.

Susanna, thank you … beyond the call of duty. Your constant chasing has been essential, only this time you saw through my tricks!

Liz, thank you again for an amazing job. We always have a laugh and I'm still convinced you're a frustrated make-up artist! Thank you for understanding.

# index